COBOL

COBOL FOR BEGINNERS

Andy Vickler

Table of Contents

Introduction

COBOL is an early programming language initially developed in 1959. It was designed to handle input for large business corporations and government agencies, which required complex calculations that were tedious for humans to complete manually. COBOL programs are still used today by various businesses, banks, insurers, and other organizations. The COBOL programming language has undergone several revisions since its creation. It was most recently standardized in 2002 by the Object Management Group (OMG).

The most commonly programmed COBOL dialect today is COBOL 2002, but there are many other dialects of the language available. COBOL 2002 is the language used by IBM think Pads, Sun Microsystems systems, and the JAWS virtual assistant program. It was also used in versions of Microsoft SQL Server from the 1990s until 2008, although it was no longer supported in later versions.

COBOL literally stands for Common Business Oriented Language. COBOL was created in 1959 by John Backus, and was primarily designed to be a language suitable for business use. The language was originally called Backus-Naur Formalism, but that name has fallen into disuse. 'COBOL' is in common use today to refer to the language itself, and its dialects are often referred to as 'COBOL languages.'

Most modern COBOL compilers have an integrated development environment (IDE) that allows the programmer to edit and compile their code directly within the program. This is convenient for programmers since they do not need to manually compile and transfer their files to another software program upon completion. COBOL programming language features a block structure that contains sections for declarations, procedures, and data structures, where all three are differentiated by a standard indentation scheme.

The standardization of COBOL occurred during the phase when the American National Standards Institute (ANSI) was developing the programming language FORTRAN, which later became the language COBOL most resembled. In fact, in 1963, John W. Backus (the inventor of FORTRAN) claimed that "the overlap between FORTRAN and COBOL is becoming greater and greater as time goes on," with some packages being 85–90% identical.

A number of examples and tutorials for COBOL exist on the Internet and are freely downloadable from various sources. The examples provided in this article are for informational purposes only. They are not meant to be used as step-by-step guides to programming and should not be used as such.

Chapter 1

Cobol Language Basics

COBOL represents Common Business Oriented Language and is an extremely famous language still being used in the monetary and authoritative frameworks of different associations. COBOL was first indicated by a gathering of three government organizations and six PC producers in the United States. COBOL has been being used since the late fifties is as yet advancing, attributable to its ubiquity among the client local area.

Language Features

The COBOL programming language has 31 divisions, 18 chapters, and 10 appendices. The divisions are: introduction, environment division, character division, numeric division, data division (also referred to as file organization), input-output procedures (IOP), sequential procedures (SP), parallel and partitioned operations (PPOPS), facilities reference summary (FRSUM), index (INDX) and examples of syntax.

What Is a Programming Language?

Programming languages are a way of getting computers to do different tasks automatically.

Programming With COBOL

COBOL syntax gives the programmer a great deal of freedom as to how statements are written and what rules must be followed. COBOL statements can be written using upper- or lowercase letters, and no spaces or other special characters are required between the words that make up a statement. Each statement must end with a semicolon (;) to denote its end.

Control Blocs and Statements

Data entry screens in a modern-day COBOL programming language are usually created using Classic ASP (Active Server Pages), which is the most popular server-side technology for creating and editing web forms. Some Web development companies, such as BI Development Solutions, have an in-house team of programmers who use a combination of ASP and COBOL

5

to create forms built on local share databases, LDAP directories or reading flat files imported into databases.

The following example shows a COBOL program written in a block style structure to illustrate how easy it is to read:

```
~~~CODE
IDENTIFICATION DIVISION.
AUTHOR. A sample program for hello world
PROGRAM-ID. HELLO. ~~~CODE
PROGRAM-ID. HELLO.
ENVIRONMENT DIVISION.
INPUT-OUTPUT SECTION.
PROGRAM-ID. HELLO
DATA SECTIONII.
$1='HELLO'I>$9>
STORAGE SECTIONIIIIIII. ~~~CODE
```

COBOL software is often called either COB, COBOL, or COBOL.

Programming Environment

In order to develop programs in COBOL, one must first install the COBOL compiler. A number of different compilers are available for download from various websites, including accenture.com. There are also a few different versions and dialects of COBOL available, such as Object Oriented (OOC) and Free form (FFT), with each having varying syntax and capabilities.

At the outset, programmers can decide whether or not to use an Integrated Development Environment (IDE). An IDEs allow the user to develop and compile their programs within the same program interface. This is convenient for programmers because it eliminates the need to compile and transfer files to another software program after programming. IDEs also act as a source code editor, allowing programmers to view and edit their programs while they are running. This is useful for testing routines, examining values of variables at run-time, and fixing bugs in a program before executing it.

The official definition of COBOL states that it is "a comprehensive, structured, and natural language designed for business application programs." It was designed to be an English-like language that could be used across business and government agencies.

COBOL can be split into four main components:

    1. Data declaration section (with 10 divisions)

    2. Procedure division (with 11 divisions)

    3. Statements division (with 11 divisions)

    4. Miscellaneous division (with 4 divisions)

Data declaration section:

    7. Character division (with 3 divisions)

    8. Numeric division (with 12 divisions)

    9. Datatype Division (with 5 divisions)

    10. Option Division (with 2 divisions)

11. Constant division (with 2 divisions)

12. Data transfer division (with 2 divisions)

13. Working-Storage Section (with 2 divisions)

Procedure division:

21. Sequential Procedure Division (with 6 divisions)

22. Linkage Section (with 1 division)

23. Alternate Procedure Division (with 4 divisions)

24. Exception Handling (with 4 divisions)

25. Entry Subroutine Group (with 10 divisions)

26. Exit Subroutine Group (with 3 divisions)

27. Procedure-Division Group (with 1 division)

28. Miscellaneous Procedure Division (with 2 divisions)

29. Entry-Response Section (with 1 division)

30. Exit-Application Section (with 1 division)

31. Working-Storage Section (with 2 divisions)

32. Interfacility Communication Section (with 2 divisions)

33. Miscellaneous Section (with 6 divisions)

34. External-Formal-Pseudo procedure Division (with 7 divisions)

35. External-Procedure Division (with 1 division)

36. External-Subprogram Division (with 2 divisions)

37. Class Subdivision (with 4 divisions)

38. Class-Subprogram Division (with 1 division)

39. Miscellaneous Section (with 6 divisions)

40. Optional Parameters Section ()

41. Termination Indication Group (with 1 division)

42. Return Value Group (with 5 divisions)

43. Comments Division (with 14 divisions)

44. Loop Statement (with 1 division)

45. Options Division (with 2 divisions)

46. Numeric-Control Statement (with 1 division)

47. Batch-Control Statement (with 1 division)

48. Default Statement (with 2 divisions)

49. Exit Subroutine Division (with 4 divisions)

50. Temporary-Storage Section ()

51. Working Storage Section ()

52. Working-Storage Section (with 2 divisions)

53. Package Division (with 1 division)

54. Listing Subdivision (with 1 division)

Three types of COBOL programs exist:

A program that contains "no executable statements", only includes comments, and no other sections. A blank line is also allowed within a program; this is called a blank statement. The first line after the opening comment block is called the block return or block exit, or simply return clause.

A program that contains executable statements but no "exit" statements. It does not include the "end" block of a program (unless it is an exit procedure that merely starts another procedure).

A program that has an execution block at the end, followed by a code sequence. It may or may not have an "end" statement, depending on whether the end subprogram is in the execution block or if it's following another subprogram. The first line after the return statement or exit procedure is called the out-block.

A program that has a return statement, and no other sections. This type of program is similar to a BEGIN statement, but not so common in COBOL programs as a BEGIN statement is. A program can have any number of exit procedures that could serve as the "end" statement, or they can be in an end block with another procedure.

A program that has only one statement. Any number of statements may be placed within this section, if the programmer feels that it is necessary. Statements are separated by a semi-colon (;) when they begin a new line, and have nothing at the end of the statement.

The other main sections are:

Variables

Local variables may only be used in procedures. Variables are delimited with '$' followed by the name and data type. For example, A3; would be an assignment to the variable A for an integer value, 3. Similar syntax is used for strings and arrays; however, variants can be changed within a procedure as well. COBOL allows the use of long strings, but restricts their size to 2GBs or 2^{30} bytes (approximately 264GBs).

Data types

COBOL has five data types: integer (signed and unsigned), short integer, long integer, floating-point and fixed-point. Variants can also be used in variables.

COBOL also allows for a variant that is 8 bytes long for small integers (less than 32 bits), which improves performance by avoiding expensive bit twiddling operations. The 8-byte small int is supported in COBOL II.

The data types are specified by the first character of each variable or field. An integer field can be specified with the optional letter 'i' in the first character.

Depending on the number of bytes used, COBOL supports data sizes from 2 to 8 bytes in length. These data sizes may be allocated smaller than the default size, such as an 8-byte integer being allocated a 7-byte size to save space for other variables.

Procedures and Functions

COBOL allows for subprograms and functions (functions in COBOL II).

Code section and work division sections

These sections contain executable code or subprograms, respectively. They may be nested to any level.

Scope of variables and constants

Variables and constants can be defined in any section, but are active only within the section they were declared.

All numeric data is fixed length. (Variable-length numeric fields are provided by the optional COBOL 2002 syntax.) The "kind" of data to be used can be declared in both the DIMENSION and DATA DIVISION definitions, for example: codice_3.

Uninitialized data elements are initialized to a null ("zeroed") value of the declared item. Variables that have not been assigned a value are automatically initialized to zero (or a null string if they are string variables). This was particularly handy with older systems that had no disk storage. The ease with which strings can be used in COBOL makes it easy to code and debug, as well as make changes; it is one of the most critical elements of the language. Strings may be up to 255 characters long.

A few data items in COBOL are classified as structured data items. They are organized into a hierarchy of levels and sublevels. The first item in the hierarchy is called the root item and is referenced by a name in all other levels of the hierarchy. Sublevel items can be accessed by specifying their parent root level and the position of a sublevel item. For example, the COBOL declaration of codice_4 would reference all items below the root item codice_5.

"Compound literals" are literals that can be written out in the source code as a specified sequence of characters, or a word in which each character is preceded by its numerical value. The data type and size restrictions are the same as for other literals.

Chapter 2

Command Line Interface

```
* internal XML or external
* external is needed when running in static mode
*
* @var boolean
*/
define('PSI_INTERNAL_XML', false);

if (version_compare("5.2", PHP_VERSION, ">")) {
    die("PHP 5.2 or greater is required!!!");
}
if (!extension_loaded("pcre")) {
    die("phpSysInfo requires the pcre extension to php in order to work
        properly.");
}

require_once APP_ROOT.'/includes/autoloader.inc.php';

// Load configuration
require_once APP_ROOT.'/config.php';

if (!defined('PSI_CONFIG_FILE') || !defined('PSI_DEBUG')) {
    $tpl = new Template("/templates/html/error_config.html");
    echo $tpl->fetch();
    die();
```

The COBOL II programming language allows you to use both interactive, procedural, and object-oriented languages such as C, C++, Ada or BASIC programming languages, in addition to the traditional COBOL language. You may use the command line interface or library features of all these languages.

COBOL is a programming language with a simple syntax for all data types. It is an interpreted, step-by-step, statement-based language, with an optional declaration area to specify the types of all variables and their values. The language consists of two parts: the COBOL source code and the "CODE" section which can be called from a tool like Visual COBOL or Visual Basic. The CODE block contains a series of statements that will be compiled into machine code as part of the program execution. The CODE block generally specifies one or more functions which will be compiled into bytecodes, JVM bytecodes, or CIL bytecodes. If there is only one function in the CODE block, it will be a subroutine and is called a procedure in COBOL-80.

A statement block can contain a sequence of statements and ends with an end-of-statement symbol: codice_10 (codice_11). The end-of-statement symbol can only be used once in a given block and is usually added to the last statement.

COBOL supports several kinds of statements.

Character manipulation functions are frequently used in COBOL programming. Some of the more useful ones include:

COBOL II supports several different methods for input and output, including COBOL's INPUT and OUTPUT statements are threaded. The two sets of input and output statements can be mixed. The fields in the DIMENSION statement are threaded; you can insert a statement in any open field. For example: The COBOL compiler does not enforce the width or length of any of these fields.

COBOL includes a number of keywords that define a variety of identifiers, such as PROCEDURE, FUNCTION, WORKING-STORAGE, etc., and these need not be spelled out.

The "CODE" section consists of COBOL statements that are compiled into machine code as part of the program execution. COBOL statements can be divided broadly into two groups:

end-of-paragraph statements, and end-of-sentence statements.

COBOL does not support constructs like if, else or for.

Like other programming languages, COBOL has statements (if, while, for, etc.) and functions (e.g., min (), max (), sqrt()) that perform specific tasks. In addition to these standard functions and the math functions performed by mathematical libraries such as math52.dll, COBOL has its own extension libraries, such as date-time library that enables date handling in COBOL programs.

"FUNCTIONAL-DOMAIN-" Following the "MODULE-ID." and a "FUNCTIONAL-DOMAIN-" string is a list of module references by name. If a module is called by reference, the second word in the list must be that module's name. The first word in the list is always a valid reference to another module, and can be used to control access to other modules at higher levels of modules. This can be used to define subroutines, data, and modules that cannot be accessed by other modules, in order to keep all program code together for ease of maintenance.

"ENTRY." is a reference to the beginning of a FORTRAN program.

"MODULE." is the name of the module containing the entry point. When modules are called by reference or by name, they are referred to by "MODULE-" plus any previous module references as specified in

"FUNCTIONAL-DOMAIN-" (see above).

"EXIT." is a reference to the end of a FORTRAN program.

"*DEVELOPMENT." This is where program comments are written.

"*SOURCE." The source code file name.

"*X10". A subroutine called to create the X10 input file and template data files.

The following example shows how this section may be used to define an X10 device subroutine.

"DEFINE EXTERNAL SUBROUTINE X10."

"SUBROUTINE X10."

"INPUT-OUTPUT SUBROUTINE."

"MODIFY OUTPUT FILES FROM STANDARD-OUTPUT.

END "EXTERNAL SUBROUTINE X10."

The "PARAMETER DIVISION" contains the parameters of the program.

The following is a typical format of the "MODULE-ID" section. It is used in the "SIMPLE" program.

"MODULE-ID." SIMPLE.

"DATA DIVISION."

"WORKING-STORAGE SECTION."

"01 InputFile pic x(17).

As you can see from the example, the format of each parameter is "MODULE.ID.". The ID is the name of the file that contains the parameters for that module (that is, "SIMPLE" in this case). Each file contains a "01" line that lists each parameter it contains. By changing the id number, more than one file can be used to define program parameters. Parameter files are not necessary, but they are useful in keeping all program parameters together. All parameters are separated by the colon character."

"01 CurrentData pic 9(5)9.

"*DISPLAY OF SIMPLE CURSOR- MOVING- COUNTER WORTH '1000'"

Note that in this case, items like the "01" line for the parameter InputFile, and even number format for value fields are desired to be specified in this section (rather than as outside comments). Such details are specified in the "MODIFY INPUT FILES FROM STANDARD-INPUT" section.

The following section is used to define the program parameters. It can be used in conjunction with the "MODIFY INPUT FILES FROM STANDARD-INPUT."

"MODULE.-ID." SIMPLE.

"DATA DIVISION."

"WORKING-STORAGE SECTION."

"01 InputFile pic x(17).

"01 CurrentData pic 9(5)9.

"*DISPLAY OF SIMPLE CURSOR- MOVING- COUNTER WORTH '1000'"

The "DATA DIVISION" is used to define data items the program will use.

"01 InputFile pic x(17).

"01 CurrentData pic 9(5)9.

The "WORKING STORAGE SECTION" contains variables that are used by the program.

"WORKING-STORAGE SECTION."

"01 InputFile pic x(17).

"01 CurrentData pic 9(5)9.

The "Section COMMON" is used to define data items that can be used throughout the program. It is used to define any subroutines or common files (input or output) that are needed by the program. This can be used in conjunction with "SELECT.", "INPUT-OUTPUT

SUBROUTINE.MODIFY INPUT FILES FROM STANDARD-INPUT", and "MODIFY OUTPUT FILES FROM STANDARD-OUTPUT".

"Section COMMON."

"01 InputFile pic x(17).

"01 CurrentData pic 9(5)9.

The common (or module) data can be used from "SELECT.MODIFY OUTPUT FILES FROM STANDARD-OUTPUT" or from the "MODIFY OUTPUT FILES FROM STANDARD-OUTPUT".

The "SELECT." section is used to select data items at the terminal.

"SELECT."

"01 InputFile pic x(17).

"01 CurrentData pic 9(5)9.

The "INPUT-OUTPUT SUBROUTINE.MODIFY INPUT FILES FROM STANDARD-INPUT" section is used to read input data from a file.

"INPUT-OUTPUT SUBROUTINE."

"MODIFY INPUT FILES FROM STANDARD-INPUT."

"01 InputFile pic x(17).

The "MODIFY OUTPUT FILES FROM STANDARD-OUTPUT section is used to write output data to a file.

"MODIFY OUTPUT FILES FROM STANDARD-OUTPUT."

"01 OutputFile pic x(17).

The "SECTION COMMON" section is used to define any subroutines or common files (input or output) that are needed by the program. This can be used in conjunction with "SELECT.", "INPUT-OUTPUT SUBROUTINE. MODIFY INPUT FILES FROM STANDARD-INPUT", "MODIFY OUTPUT FILES FROM STANDARD-OUTPUT".

"SECTION COMMON."

"01 InputFile pic x(17).

"01 CurrentData pic 9(5)9.

The "MODIFY INPUT FILES FROM STANDARD-INPUT." section is used to read input data from a file.

"MODIFY INPUT FILES FROM STANDARD-INPUT."

"01 InputFile pic x(17).

The "MODIFY OUTPUT FILES FROM STANDARD-OUTPUT." section is used to write output data to a file.

"MODIFY OUTPUT FILES FROM STANDARD-OUTPUT. "

"01 OutputFile pic x(17).

The "SECTION COMMON" section is used to define any subroutines or common files (input or output) that are needed by the program. This can be used in conjunction with "SELECT.", "INPUT-OUTPUT SUBROUTINE.MODIFY INPUT FILES FROM STANDARD-INPUT", "MODIFY OUTPUT FILES FROM STANDARD-OUTPUT".

The "SECTION COMMON." section is used to define any subroutines or common files (input or output) that are needed by the program. This can be used in conjunction with 'SELECT.", "INPUT-OUTPUT SUBROUTINE.MODIFY INPUT FILES FROM STANDARD-INPUT", "MODIFY OUTPUT FILES FROM STANDARD-OUTPUT".

The "SUBROUTINE" section is used to define subroutines. It can be used in conjunction with 'SELECT.", "INPUT-OUTPUT SUBROUTINE.MODIFY INPUT FILES FROM STANDARD-INPUT", and 'MODIFY OUTPUT FILES FROM STANDARD-OUTPUT'.

The "SUBROUTINE" section is used as an "INPUT-OUTPUT SUBROUTINE."" It can be used in conjunction with 'SELECT.MODIFY OUTPUT FILES FROM STANDARD-OUTPUT' and 'MODIFY INPUT FILES FROM STANDARD-INPUT'.

The following section can be used to define any subroutines that the program will use. It is useful in keeping all program subroutines together.

"SUBROUTINE."

END "SUBROUTINE."

The "EXCEPTION-CONTROL". section is used to specify the possible error conditions that can be encountered by the program. It is used in conjunction with the "DISPLAY ERROR CONDITIONS". It can be used in conjunction with 'SELECT.", 'INPUT-OUTPUT SUBROUTINE.MODIFY INPUT FILES FROM STANDARD-INPUT', 'MODIFY OUTPUT FILES FROM STANDARD-OUTPUT'

The "EXCEPTION-CONTROL." section is used to specify the possible error conditions. It can be used in conjunction with 'SELECT.', 'INPUT-OUTPUT SUBROUTINE.MODIFY INPUT FILES FROM STANDARD-INPUT', 'MODIFY OUTPUT FILES FROM STANDARD-OUTPUT'.

The "DISPLAY ERROR CONDITIONS" section is used in conjunction with the "EXCEPTION-CONTROL." section. It can be used in conjunction with 'SELECT.," 'INPUT-OUTPUT SUBROUTINE.MODIFY INPUT FILES FROM STANDARD-INPUT', 'MODIFY OUTPUT FILES FROM STANDARD-OUTPUT"

The following sections can be used to specify additional, optional clauses for the program. They are used in conjunction with the "MODIFY INPUT FILES FROM STANDARD-INPUT." section, and "MODIFY OUTPUT FILES FROM STANDARD-OUTPUT" section.

The "DISPLAY ERROR CONDITIONS" section is used to display error conditions. It can be used in conjunction with the 'SELECT.", 'INPUT-OUTPUT SUBROUTINE.MODIFY INPUT FILES FROM STANDARD-INPUT', 'MODIFY OUTPUT FILES FROM STANDARD-OUTPUT'

The "SUBROUTINE" section is used to define subroutines that the program will use. It can be used in conjunction with 'SELECT.", 'INPUT-OUTPUT SUBROUTINE.MODIFY INPUT FILES FROM STANDARD-INPUT', 'MODIFY OUTPUT FILES FROM STANDARD-OUTPUT'.

The "SUBROUTINE" section is used as an "INPUT-OUTPUT SUBROUTINE."" It can be used in conjunction with 'SELECT.MODIFY OUTPUT FILES FROM STANDARD-OUTPUT' and 'MODIFY INPUT FILES FROM STANDARD-INPUT'.

This is a simple program that reads input from standard input, prints the input on standard output, and prints the terminating character on standard error.

A program that reads from its standard input, prints on standard output and returns the input on standard error. It was found to be too hard to implement in the general case. See "Display Error Conditions" subsection of this example.

An example that reads from its standard input, prints on standard output and returns the input on standard error.

The "READ-FROM STANDARD INPUT", "PRINT OUTPUT", and "RETURN INPUT TO STANDARD ERROR" sections are used in conjunction with the SELECT.

The "INPUT-OUTPUT SUBROUTINE.READ FROM STANDARD INPUT" section is used to read input data, and can be used in conjunction with the SELECT.

"INPUT-OUTPUT SUBROUTINE."

"READ FROM STANDARD INPUT."

The "INPUT-OUTPUT SUBROUTINE." section is used as an "INPUT-OUTPUT SUBROUTINE."" It can be used in conjunction with 'SELECT.MODIFY OUTPUT FILES FROM STANDARD-OUTPUT' and 'MODIFY INPUT FILES FROM STANDARD-INPUT'.

The following sections can be used to specify additional, optional clauses for the program. They are used in conjunction with the "MODIFY INPUT FILES FROM STANDARD-INPUT." section, and "MODIFY OUTPUT FILES FROM STANDARD-OUTPUT" section.

The "DISPLAY ERROR CONDITIONS" section is used to display error conditions. It can be used in conjunction with the 'SELECT.''' and 'INPUT-OUTPUT SUBROUTINE.MODIFY INPUT FILES FROM STANDARD-INPUT'.

The "SUBROUTINE" section is used to define subroutines that the program will use. It can be used in conjunction with 'SELECT.", 'INPUT-OUTPUT SUBROUTINE.MODIFY INPUT FILES FROM STANDARD-INPUT', 'MODIFY OUTPUT FILES FROM STANDARD-OUTPUT'.

The following sections can be used to specify additional, optional clauses for the program. They are used in conjunction with the "MODIFY OUTPUT FILES FROM STANDARD-OUTPUT." section, and "MODIFY INPUT FILES FROM STANDARD-INPUT" section.

The "DISPLAY ERROR CONDITIONS" section is used to display error conditions. It can be used in conjunction with the 'SELECT.", 'INPUT-OUTPUT SUBROUTINE.

COBOL was implemented using machine coding, which was an archaic method of code development in 1959. In 1967, COBOL II was developed as a more modern implementation, and made use of high-level languages to implement COMPUTATIONAL statements previously handled machine code. Since then, many versions have been created and implemented with varying capabilities; one such example is COBOL-85.

Chapter 3

Interfacing With Other Languages and Databases

COBOL has proven difficult to interface with "modern" languages like Java and C++, due to the former's tendency to use pointers and the latter's use of C-style typedefs. This is mainly because COBOL was designed in an era when data represented by numbers stored in computer memory was assumed to be an integer or character (such as 00000111) rather than a full data type (such as decimal number 17.3) that may contain both values. Therefore, imprecise data types are often used in COBOL programs for variables.

COBOL implements environment variables using the % symbol rather than a dollar sign as is common in Unix/Linux systems. This means that Unix and Linux shells do not support environment variables correctly when they contain % characters. The solution is to use double quotation marks around the value (i.e., "NAME" instead of NAME).

The biggest drawback to COBOL is the lack of object orientation. Object-oriented design was well established by the end of COBOL's lifespan, and it was therefore more practical to convert a program written in COBOL into one written in an object-oriented language such as Visual Basic.NET, C++, or Java. COBOL is not capable of performing inheritance, but it still uses subroutines, and there are ways to perform many object-oriented tasks.

A much-cited example of a COBOL legacy system is the LexisNexis legal research service. LexisNexis maintains over 1.5 petabytes of legal documents, including case law and statutes, which is accessible through its mainframe computer systems.

The United States Internal Revenue Service uses COBOL to process tax returns and related filings.

COBOL is used in the financial services industry to create applications for customer-centric functions such as account management and loan origination and servicing.

COBOL is used by a large number of corporations, government agencies, and other organizations to write business applications. In particular, COBOL is used by many banks, capital markets firms and government agencies which rely on mainframe computers.

According to the latest figures from IDC (June 2016), IBM one-year maintenance contracts for a mainframe-based COBOL application cost between $2.8 and $3.9 million per year. This compares with $1.4 to $2 for Java and .NET applications running on distributed systems.

In 2008, a survey of hundreds of software developers commissioned by SSI Group revealed that COBOL was used in 22 per cent of all systems, making it more popular than the next two most widely used languages, Java and C++.

In the early 1990s, a few companies began offering open source COBOL compilers that translated COBOL applications into modern programming languages such as C++ or Java. While clearly relevant to corporations that cannot afford to rewrite their legacy applications with new technologies, these compilers have not benefitted from the widespread availability of low-cost computing.

One problem's particularity is its size. COBOL programs (written in the 1970s and 1980s) become large, complex, and unwieldy after a while.

COBOL programs are prone to errors which may overwhelm a computer system. Not being object-oriented, they do not lend themselves readily to static checking of program logic.

This problem is compounded by the slowness of COBOL compilers to handle complex code. Even very simple loops or decision statements are often coded inefficiently. On a modern computer, this will lead to an exponential increase in the time required to run a COBOL application. The resulting data loss may force companies to shut down their systems at crucial moments and even cause serious financial losses if unforeseen safety problems necessitate a software rollback.

COBOL programs are often difficult to understand without outside documentation, especially for programmers that are not familiar with the language; it uses conventions and variables used in other languages (the use of character variables for string constants, for example). The same is true for subroutine calls.

This can lead to errors and bugs that are hard to spot (such as confusion between parameters and control-statements, or between a parameter and the function name leading to an infinite loop).

Notes:

COBOL programs are often difficult to read. For example, they usually consist of many subroutines with their own variables and routines. Reading one of these may require detailed knowledge of other routines and the variables used in them. This makes it hard for non-programmers to debug COBOL programs. Another problem is the lack of standard input/output modules (the use of all-purpose functions such as GET, SAVE, SELECT, and PRINT to handle input/output).

The lack of object orientation also makes it hard to read and understand code, as well as facilitates the creation of code that is very difficult to maintain and extend. In a structured language such as C or Java, one can freely use the power of inheritance and other object-oriented techniques to create re-usable classes and templates. This is not possible in COBOL (without resorting to advanced techniques such as multiple inheritance).

One reason for the adoption of COBOL was its low implementation cost compared with higher level languages such as Fortran. This meant that businesses could afford more computing power at lower initial investment. Although the difference between the lowest cost equipment for most of the production period was much smaller, a large number of COBOL applications were still being developed by small- and medium-sized companies; so implementation costs for these applications are significantly higher than for applications written in other languages. These costs are also significantly higher in the U.S., where smaller businesses have less access to finance and can therefore purchase fewer computers while having their software development projects completed more slowly and more expensively. The result is that modern COBOL can be prohibitively expensive when implemented on inexpensive hardware such as mainframes, which are used largely by businesses with lower revenues but longer life-cycle profit margins and lower core costs per unit of capacity.

COBOL has been ported to most computer hardware, operating systems and mainframe software environments. It can be used in both on-line (interactive) and batch environments, on mainframes, as well as mini and micro computers.

Because of its commercial importance and dominance throughout the 1960s–1980s, it is supported by a number of vendors both in terms of compilers, runtime libraries, and other tools to facilitate development for platforms that may lack native support for COBOL. In addition, there are also open-source implementations of the COBOL syntax written in recent years for use with Linux and Microsoft Windows operating systems.

Due to its legacy, COBOL is still used in several commercial financial applications, especially in the insurance and banking sectors. This is due to the limitations of modern languages for this sector, such as C++, that may be more suited for programming programmer tools.

The rise of Web 2.0 has led to increased interest in COBOL for new applications on the internet. In addition, web technologies such as XML make it possible to use a subset of COBOL in web applications that previously could not be developed using only traditional programming languages. HTML forms can be built using Forms development tools created with an XML schema that provides a component-based architecture and enables reuse and reusability of components between applications. Part of the Forms specification is an XML schema that defines the Forms elements and attributes to be used in the development of web applications.

However, despite this, the semantics of COBOL make it hard to combine with other programming languages (including ones descended from C) without major changes.

COBOL can be used to develop software for small or large systems, for use on a single machine, or distributed over many machines. It can be used on a single machine as a batch processor or in an interactive mode using terminals, teletypewriters, or workstations.

COBOL programs can be run on a mainframe or mini-computer, significant changes being required for the latter case. Some of these are also needed in order to migrate to a non-mainframe system, since most mainframes support multiple operating systems, each with different environments and standards. For example, IBM's Data I/O Facility allows COBOL programmers to write code that can be run on a workstation using AutoCAD or other drawing tools. It is also possible to use tools such as the OLE DB Database Administrator (ODBA) library with COBOL applications written in Visual Basic .NET. This allows COBOL programs to be run in an environment with a graphical user interface and no mainframe.

There are also changes required when moving to the Windows NT environment; for example, many of the utilities provided by IBM are only available on Windows NT. There are also differences between COBOL in the various environments, since some standards have changed over time and not all platforms support all standards. The year 2000 solution is required for batch files, since there can be problems with date formats as well as fixed length fields. Since batch files cannot easily accommodate these changes, it may be necessary to rewrite them completely. COBOL programs for interactive use may need slightly different changes than batch files.

As of 2006, the latest version of COBOL is 2002 from ISO and ANSI. The 2002 Amendment 1 is available as an addendum to the standard, although it is mentioned that it has no official status. There are also two addenda for microcomputer programs (1987) and for reports (1995). There is also ISO/IEC 1989, which defines how COBOL should be used in seven specific domains: Office Systems, Banking and Finance, Telecommunications and Data Communications, Manufacturing Systems, Petroleum Refining Systems, Transport Scheduling Systems, and Travel Reservation System.

COBOL compilers may generate an object code in any of several formats. The most important of these are Micro Focus Intercal, a native code format that is portable across operating systems and processor platforms, and the Unix-based VMS Assembler II, which is used in system programming.

The following is a simple example of COBOL source code:

This code can be compiled into either a mainframe executable or a virtual machine executable. It can also be compiled into Java bytecode.

The sample shows the "screen division" structure of COBOL programs (see the section on Syntax). The division into record structure makes COBOL a so-called "structured" language, as opposed to many "unstructured" languages such as C or Perl.

Structured languages such as COBOL are more amenable to programming by writing "screenfuls" of code, generally placed in a form similar to that shown above.

The screen division structure enables the programmer to directly manipulate the screen. The "PROMPT" statement is used to show a visual prompt on the screen. This is used in connection with other input/output commands which will be discussed later in this article.

In the example that follows, a simple spreadsheet application has been written. It is known as an "interactive COBOL program", since the user can enter data interactively and the application will run its commands for editing those records.

One of the simplest interactive applications is one that will read a sequence of numeric or alphanumeric data items from the keyboard and then calculate some function of them. This can be done using an "alter table" command to add successive values to a running total. (Other COBOL subprograms are used for the arithmetic operations.)

Chapter 4

Introduction to Programming Concepts

Fundamental Programming Concepts

Programming is essentially about solving problems. You write lines of code to save the world. Each program you write must satisfy a specific need, which eventually makes work easier. Before you set out to write a program, you must first understand the issue at hand.

Ask yourself what you are trying to solve. One of the best things about using computers is that they are programmed to solve repetitive assignments. Take calculations, for example. You can use your calculator and work out answers to a given series of problems. It might take you a long time, but you will get it done eventually. However, with your computer, all you need is to create a formula and work out all the answers in seconds.

Most problems have more than one possible solution. Some solutions are longer, others are shorter. However, at the end of the day you have an answer. Through programming, you solve problems in the shortest possible way. Programming is about useful resource allocation. You save time solving problems through the programs you write instead of going about them the manual way.

Computer programs are nothing more than a set of instructions that perform a unique instruction when instructed by the computer. There are two different forms of programming, structured programming, and object-oriented programming.

Structured programming is a model where you run codes in sequence. This model includes control statements that determine the codes that apply in the sequence. Structured programming focuses on improving quality, clarity, and the time to development of any computer program.

Object-oriented programming on the other hand is a model composed of objects whose data include methods, attributes, and procedures. Objects interact independently, sharing messages as opposed to structured programming where there is a strict sequence.

Program Structure

All structured programs have the same overall pattern, which includes statements that indicate where the program begins, the variable declaration, and blocks of code that represent the program statements.

In the example below, you see a representation of the fabled Hello World in different programming languages. Whichever language you use, the program will print Hello World on your screen.

```
Basicprint "Hello World"
Perl#!/usr/local/bin/perl - w print "Hello
World";
Javaclass helloworld {
public static void main (String args[]) {
System.out.println ("Hello World");
}
}
Oracle PL/SQL CREATE OR REPLACE PROCEDURE
helloworld AS BEGIN
DBMS_OUTPUT.PUT_LINE('Hello World');
END;
Pascalprogram helloworld (output);
begin
writeln('Hello World');
end.
C#include <stdio.h>
void main () {
printf("Hello World");}
```

Your program is either poorly structured or well-structured. In a well-structured program, you can see an organized division of components while this is not present in a poorly structured program. Well-structured programs also use appropriate program units and data structures, each of which has a single entry and exit point. Poorly structured programs feature arbitrary flow of control and data structures.

Variable Declaration

A variable is a symbolic name that is assigned some information. It is a reference point. The name assigned to a variable represents the information it holds. Information represented by variables is dynamic. As a result, the information might change from time to time. However, the operations associated with the variable will not. Variables are storage locations and symbolic names that hold some information or quantity with a value.

Variables are the foundation of all programs and program languages. They help you store information which can be retrieved for use later on. For retrieval, the user simply refers to a word that describes the information.

Say you visit a website and find a small text box that asks for your name. That text box represents a variable. If the developer named the box client Name, this would be the symbolic name for the variable.

Therefore, if you write your name in that box, the information you key in is stored in a client Name variable. If the developer requests the value that the client Name variable holds, the information you typed into that box is displayed.

There are different types of variables, including the following:

String – refers to a collection of characters.

Character – unitary character like a punctuation mark or an alphabetic letter.

Float – also referred to as real. Means to store fractional or real numbers.

Integer – to store whole numbers or integers.

Variables are further grouped into five categories as follows:

NB: The examples below is how it is done in Ruby programming language. The concept is however same for all major programming languages.

- **Constants**

When writing a program, you must declare constants by capitalizing the first letters in the name of the variable. Constants store data that you might not need to change. By default, most programming languages other than Ruby do not permit value changes to constants. However, just because Ruby allows you to change constant variables does not mean that you should.

This is what a constant variable looks like:

```
1 | MY_CONSTANT = 'I am reachable throughout
the process.'
```

• Global variables

Global variables are indicated with a dollar sign at the beginning of the variable name. They override all the boundaries and are applicable all through the app.

This is what a global variable looks like:

```
1 | $var = 'I am also reachable throughout
the process.'
```

• Class variables

Class variables must be declared with two @ signs at the beginning of the variable. They are used by different instances of a class.

This is what a class variable looks like:

```
1 | @@instances = 3
```

• Instance variables

Instance variables are declared with one @ sign. They are useful in object-oriented programming.

This is what an instance variable looks like:

```
1 | @var = 'I am available throughout the
current process.'
```

- **Local variables**

Of all variables you come across in programming, local variables are among the most frequently used. They conform to all boundary scopes. When declaring a local variable, you do not use either @ or $, neither do you need to capitalize the variable name.

This is what a local variable looks like:

```
1 | var = 'Pass me around to scope
boundaries.'
```

Looping Structures

Remember when we mentioned earlier that computers allow you to perform calculations repeatedly? This is what happens with loop structures. Loop structures enable you to repeatedly run lines of code, even if it is one line of code. The idea here is to replicate the statement within a loop structure until you meet a given condition, whether True or False.

If the code does not have a functioning exit routine, it is referred to as an infinite loop. This looping structure will persist until it is detected by the operating system and terminated. When terminated in such a manner, you receive an error. It can also terminate as a result of another event occurring, like scheduling the program to terminate after a predetermined amount of time.

Control Structures

Control structures refer to programming blocks that analyze variables and determine the best direction to proceed according to the parameters provided. From basic understanding, control structures are the decision-makers in computer programming. They determine how the computer should respond when specific parameters and conditions are upheld.

Whenever you run a program, your computer reads all the code in the same way you read a book. This is what is referred to as code flow. In the course of reading all the code, your computer might encounter a scenario where it needs to skip from one point to another, or repeat a specific part of the code to perform some activity. There are strict rules that make this possible. These rules necessitate a specific decision which affects the way code flows. The specific decision is referred to as a control structure.

Syntax

Syntax refers to the set or rules that guide the combination of symbols which are structured in a specific programming language. If you try to access a document that has the wrong syntax, you end up with a syntax error. Syntax in programming, therefore, works the same way spelling and grammar do in linguistic classes.

An English statement with poor spelling and lots of grammar mistakes is difficult, if not impossible to understand. This is the same thing that happens with syntax errors. Since your computer cannot understand the code, it cannot execute it, hence a syntax error.

Things are, however, more complicated with computers. In English, you can understand what the sentence means, especially if it has simple errors. In computer programming, the tiniest syntax error in your code will render it useless and unreadable. This is why programmers are often encouraged to focus not only on logic when writing programs, but on syntax too.

Computer programming syntax is further classified into the following:

- Words – lexical content that represent how tokens are formed from characters.

- Phrases – grammatical content that represent how phrases are formed from tokens.

Context – determinants that indicate among other things, whether types are valid, the variables that names refer to, and so forth.

Chapter 5

Data Types, Variables, and Data Structures

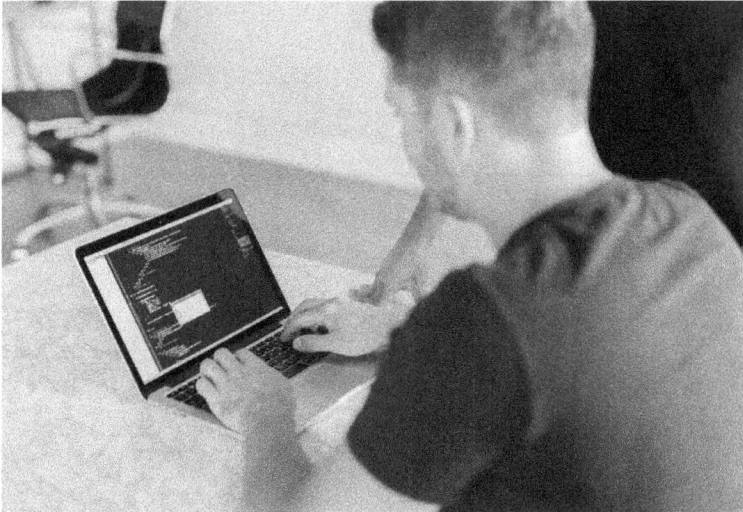

Data Types

Internal Format Data

We have defined numeric data before and we noticed that we used one byte to define one digit. When data are in this format, we say that they are in the external format. The format is described as external because when data come from the outside, say from the keyboard, they come in this format. If we consider the byte as consisting of two four-bit components, each component is able to hold a digit. In this way a byte will be able to hold two digits. When data are in this format, two digits per byte, we say that they are in the internal format.

Data in the external format are also said to be in the unpacked or display format. On the other hand, data in the internal format are said to be packed. Each format has its own usage, as shown below.

Internal Format
Usage is comp-3
Usage is computational –3
Usage is packed-decimal
External Format
Usage is display
No usage specified – default applies
Table 08.01 – Basic Numeric Formats

Comp-3 is an abbreviation of computational-3 and, not surprisingly, the extended form is seldom used. Usage is display is the default so it is normally left out. Also, the words usage is need not be coded, it being sufficient to specify the usage. The following examples depict the situation described:

```
05   W10-amt       pic S9(5)V99 usage is comp-
3.


Or


05   W10-amt       pic S9(5)V99 comp-3.
Or



05   W10-amt       pic S9(5)V99 packed-
decimal.

Or
05   W10-amt       pic S9(5)V99 computational-
3.

And

05   W10-amt       pic S9(5)V99 usage is
display.

Or
05   W10-amt       pic S9(5)V99.
```

When we pack data we must be able to determine how many bytes the data will occupy. Let us consider the previous definitions:

```
05   W10-amt           pic S9(5)V99.
05   W10-amt           pic S9(5)V99 comp-3.
```

We can see that the data in the display format will have used seven bytes. To determine the storage required by the packed data definition we have to do some arithmetic. Before we do that, however, let us see what the two definitions look like in storage.

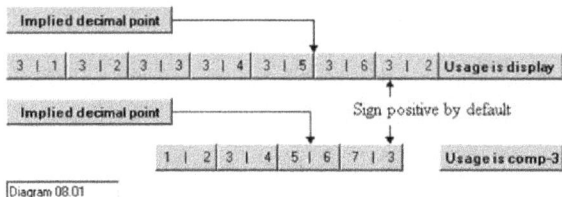

Diagram 08.01

You will recall that the high order four bits in a byte are referred to as the zone bits. The low order four bits are referred to as the digit bits. Notice that in the unpacked field the sign occupies the zone bits of the low order byte. In the packed field the sign occupies the digit bits of the low order byte. In fact, in a packed field it is as if the sign had been appended to the data. The sign follows the data.

We see that in the packed field definition we have catered for seven digits. In addition we must allow for the sign, so we have:

```
No. of digits          7

Sign                   1
Total                  8  /  2  =  4
```

The field would occupy four bytes. What if the picture for W10-amt said pic S9(6)V99? Our arithmetic would look as follows:

```
No. of digits              8
Sign                       1
Total                  9  /  2  =  4.5
```

Note, however, that we cannot have half a byte so the field would occupy five bytes. Half a byte, the zone of the high order byte would not be used. The number of digits in your definition should always be odd. Graphically the storage would look as follows:

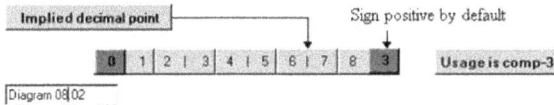

Diagram 08 02

The instruction "move 1123456.78 to W10-amt" would cause the field to contain the value: 123456.78. The program is precluded from using the zone of the high order byte. The program will consume extra cycles to ascertain what it is able to use. Consequently, make sure that you define the field in such a way that there is never half a byte unused. The preceding definition should be: pic S9(7)V99. The arithmetic would then be:

```
No. of digits              9
Sign                       1
Total            10 / 2  =  5
```

The number of digits in the definition of a packed field should always be odd.

```
(Above: 7 + 2 = 9)
```

More on the Move Statement

Moving Alphanumeric to Alphanumeric

One important point to note is that in a move, the rules that apply with respect to alignment are the rules that apply to the receiving field. Data in an alphanumeric field align on the left. Thus the first byte to be moved from the source will be the leftmost byte and it will be moved to the leftmost byte in the destination. The move will proceed byte by byte, from source to destination, until all bytes have been transferred or until all bytes in the destination have received data. In this latter case data in the destination would have been truncated. Consider the following definitions:

```
05 W10-source      pic X (04) value 'SAME'.
05 W10-dest1       pic X (07) value 'Michael'.
05 W10-dest2       pic X (03) value 'Roy'.
```

The instruction:

```
move W10-source to W10-dest1 W10-dest2
```

Graphically we have:

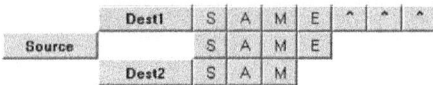

We have used the '^' to represent a space.

When the data were moved to dest1, they were aligned on the left and once all the data had been transferred, the remaining bytes were filled with spaces. In the case of Dest2, the destination is shorter than the source so the data were truncated.

Moving Numeric to Numeric

In moving a numeric source to a numeric destination, data are again moved byte by byte, but in this case, alignment is on the decimal point. If a decimal point is not present, alignment will be on the right.

If the destination is shorter than the source, the data will be truncated. If the destination field is longer than the source field, unused bytes in the destination will be zero filled.

Assume the following definitions:

```
05 source          pic S9(04) value 1234.
05 dest1           pic S9(07).
05 dest2           pic S9(03).
```

The instruction:

move source to dest1 dest2

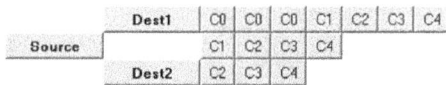

Dest1 is longer than source, the data was moved byte by byte, starting on the right, unused positions on the left were zero filled. On the other hand dest2 is shorter than source. This time truncation took place. The leftmost digit was truncated.

Let us now consider the situation where the definitions contain a decimal point. We know that alignment will be on the decimal point.

```
05 source          pic S9(03)V99 value
123.45.
05 dest1           pic S9(05)V9.
```

Graphically represented we have:

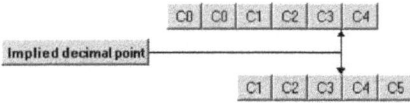

On the right there was truncation, the low order decimal position was lost. On the left the positions left blank were zero filled. The receiving field had extra integer positions and was short on the decimal positions. Example:

```
05 source          pic S9(03)V9 value 123.4.
05 dest1           pic S9(05)V99.
```

Graphically represented we have:

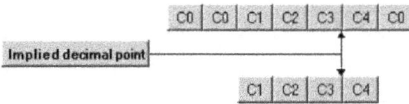

We had zero filling on the right and on the left - the bytes that did not receive data were zero filled.

Moving Alphanumeric to Numeric

Remember, in a move the rules that apply are the rules of the receiving field. The points to note are that data will be aligned on the right and that the sending field may not contain spaces. In the following definition the two rightmost positions will contain spaces. In this case there will be an attempt to move these two spaces to the receiving numeric field. This will be invalid data and the program will terminate abnormally.

```
05   alfa-num          pic X(06) pic '1234'.
```

Assume the following definitions:

```
05 alpha-num           pic X9(06) value '123456'.
05 num                 pic S9(04).
```

The instruction:

```
Move alpha-num to num
```

In moving from an alphanumeric source to a numeric destination it is the responsibility of the programmer to ensure that only valid data are moved to the destination. In the preceding example did the programmer expect 1234 to be transferred or did he expect the value 3456? We suggest that both source and destination be the same size.

Moving Numeric to Alphanumeric

The leftmost position in the numeric source will be moved to the leftmost position in the alphanumeric destination. Note also that the source may not contain a decimal point. If the source is longer than the destination there will be truncation. If the destination is longer, the unused positions on the right will be space filled.

```
05 W20-alpha-num pic X(06).
05 W20-num1      pic S9(04) value 1234.
```

The instruction:

The graphical representation:

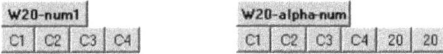

```
W20-num1
C1 C2 C3 C4
```
```
W20-alpha-num
C1 C2 C3 C4  20  20
```

We may move a packed field to an alphanumeric field as long as it does not contain decimals. The field will be unpacked into the alphanumeric field.

Moving a Group Field to a Numeric Field

You will recall that a group field behaves as an alphanumeric field. We have already said that in a move the rules followed are the rules pertaining to the receiving field. Regrettably, when it comes to the move from a group field to a numeric field this does not apply; the rules that follow are the rules for an alphanumeric destination. Assume the following definitions:

```
01 an-group                Value 1234.
    05 W20-an1   Pic X (02).
    05 W20-an2   Pic X (02).
01 nums.
    05 num1      Pic S9(04).
    05 num2      Pic S9(03).
    05 num3      Pic S9(05).
```

The instruction: move an-group to num1

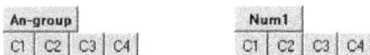

```
An-group
C1 C2 C3 C4
```
```
Num1
C1 C2 C3 C4
```

Since the two fields are the same size, the results are acceptable and execution proceeds without a hitch.

```
move an-group to num2
```

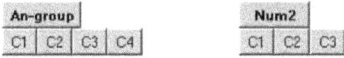

The destination is smaller than the source; truncation takes place but execution is successful.

```
move an-group to num3
```

Execution is not successful. Because the numeric field is being treated as an alphanumeric field, data are moved in starting on the left and vacant positions are space filled. When moving of a space to a numeric field is attempted, execution is interrupted and the program terminates abnormally.

Moving a Literal to an Alphanumeric Field

Moving a literal of type numeric is the same as moving a field of type numeric. The move to an alphanumeric field is permitted as long as the literal does not contain a decimal point. The definition and the instruction follow:

```
05 alpha-num              pic X (05).
move 1234 to alpha-num
```

The data were moved in accordance with alphanumeric moves. Alignment was on the left and the vacant position on the right was space filled. Had we coded the move as follows, it would have been successful. ASCII hexadecimal 2E is the decimal point

```
move '123.4' to alpha-num
```

Literal				
C1	C2	C3	2E	C4

Alpha-num				
C1	C2	C3	2E	C4

What was moved was not a numeric source but an alphanumeric source.

Moving All 'Literal'

The move transfers the named literal repeatedly to the destination field. The literal may be numeric or alphanumeric - but, if numeric, it may not be packed. The literal may consist of one or more characters. Irrespective of the type of the destination, the rules are the same as for the alphanumeric move. Assume the following definitions:

```
05 alpha-num1        pic X (06).
05 alpha-num2        pic X (07).
```

The instruction:

```
move all 'AB' to alpha-num1
```

Graphically represented:

Literal	
41	42

Alpha-num1					
41	42	41	42	41	42

The literal was moved repeatedly, starting on the left, until the destination was full. Let us now see what will happen if the size of the destination is not a multiple of the size of the literal.

The instruction:

```
move all 'AB' to alpha-num2
```

Graphically represented:

Literal	
41	42

Alpha-num2						
41	42	41	42	41	42	41

Transfer stops when the last position in the destination receives a character.

Assume the following definitions:

```
05 num1          pic 9(05)V99.
```

The instruction:

```
move all '12' to num1
```

Graphically represented:

Literal	
31	32

Num1						
31	32	31	32	31	30	30

The literal was moved repeatedly, starting on the left, until the integer component was full. Transfer stopped and the decimal component was zero filled. Note that the literal must be an integer.

The Justified Clause

The justified clause is applied to elementary fields of type alphanumeric or alphabetic. The clause is used to force alignment on the right as against the natural alignment of these types on the left. The clause may be shortened. We may also specify right, as shown below:

```
05 alpha-num1        pic X (06) just.
05 alpha-num2        pic X (06) just right.
```

The instruction:

```
move 'Yes' to alpha-num1
move 'No' to alpha-num2
```

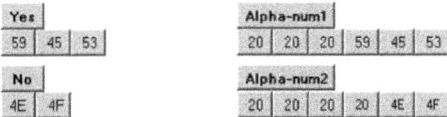

The values shown for the characters are the ASCII equivalents. The data were aligned on the right and the vacant positions were space filled. What will happen if the destination field is shorter than the literal?

```
move 'October' to alpha-num1
```

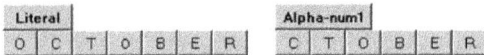

Truncation was now on the left.

If the move all 'literal' is applied to a field for which the justified clause has been specified, the justified clause will not be respected. Consider the following code:

```
05  alpha-num2          pic X(07) just right.
move all 'Yes' to alpha-num2
```

The graphical representation:

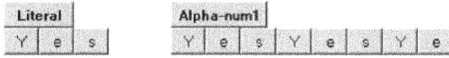

Because the last character on the right is an 'e' it follows that the first character moved was the 'Y' and it was moved to the leftmost position in the destination.

Chapter 6

Control Blocks and Statements

The block structure is a series of statements where the opening statement indent is typically 4 spaces, the contents are indented further, and the closing statement has an indentation of exactly 72 spaces. The 72-space indent tells the compiler that the program block has ended.

Function Block

The top of the function block is indented an additional 4 spaces to tell the COBOL compiler that the code within this section will call a subprogram. The closing statement for the function block is indented exactly 36 spaces, which indicates that this end of control statement has been reached and the control reverts back to the calling program.

COBOL uses indenting to differentiate between code and comments. Indented code is computer executable statements, and indented comments are what the programmer writes to explain the program to themselves and others.

A comment is introduced by an asterisk (*) followed by text written by the programmer to explain what the code does. In standard COBOL, either upper or lower case letters can be used for comments. This practice continues in most modern COBOL dialects, but older versions of COBOL required word division between the asterisk and other letters. The asterisk should be the first character on a line and be indented 4 spaces.

The start of an actual statement block is marked by an open brace ({) that has an indentation of 4 spaces. The actual statement is then indented further to 12 spaces, and each subsequent statement is indented another 12 spaces. After the last statement in a block has been displayed, the next statement will have an indentation of 72 spaces. This marks the end of the block, indicating that control has been returned to the calling program.

A procedure is a group of statements that can be executed on a single line when the procedure name is preceded with a coma (period).

Data Block

The data block is used to store variables and constants. A variable is declared by listing the data type and name, along with an initial value for that variable. Data blocks always begin with an asterisk (*), which signifies that this is the 'beginning' of the block. In some cases, the asterisk is not necessary if the 'type section' of a data block has already been defined in an outer block.

COBOL Variable

Variables in COBOL may be either "Fixed" or "Variable". A fixed variable is one whose size limits the amount of data that can be stored. Variable length data takes up more memory space than a fixed length data variable. Variable length items require the programmer to specify the length of each item, whereas fixed-length items require the programmer to know only how many bytes of storage to allocate. Typically, number and date variables are fixed-length and character variables are variable-length.

COBOL Constants

COBOL is a strongly typed language. Data types are specified for each variable that is declared. The main data types are character, numeric and date & time. SQL is available in both ANSI/ISO and IMS languages. Character data types include fixed length alphanumeric (CHARACTER), full ASCII, half-duplex numeric

(NATIONAL CHARACTER) and packed decimal (DECIMAL). Numeric variables can be either fixed- or floating-point data types. Date & time data types include DATE, TIMESTAMP and TIMESTAMP WITH TIME ZONE.

Full details of the COBOL data types are given in the section below.

Data Declarations

The "DATA DIVISION" identifies the various sections of a COBOL program and is used to define variables. Data declarations are included in the "FILE SECTION". The data section includes the following fields or 'parts' of a record:

Control than can be used with data declarations are:

Parameter declarations can be used to pass data between subprograms. Parameters can receive data in two ways, by value and by reference. When parameters are passed by value, the subprogram has a copy of the variable, rather than access to the original variable. When parameters are passed by reference, the subprogram has access to the original variable.

Immediately following the data declarations is a "DATA SEQUENCE", which specifies what type of data will be stored in the variable. The description field contains the specific name of the variable. A record can contain many data sequences, each associated with different variables. In case of a program error, the COBOL compiler is able to tell which sequence caused an error by looking at each sequence and noting what variable was assigned to (or referenced) in each part of the program.

The "CONTENTS" section defines the type of data that will be stored. The contents field IDENTIFIES the data type. The "DATA AND RESULTS" section contains any variables that will provide the data to be processed by the program, as well as any results of the processing.

The last section is an optional "A-ZERO / YES/ NO DATA SECTION". This piece of information is provided to help diagnose problems by describing what data has been stored in which variable.

A "FILE SECTION" contains information about files accessed by the program. The file section includes:

The optional "A-ZERO / YES/ NO DATA SECTION" is followed by the PROGRAM IDENTIFICATION, which lists information to help identify the program and its purpose. This section can also include additional comments to help in understanding the program's logic.

The compiler directives are found at the end of a COBOL program, before the "IDENTIFICATION DIVISION". The directives are used to help the COBOL compiler process the program.

"COBOL PROGRAM-ID." is the name of the program. It is used to identify programs in external files and in diagnostic messages.

"IDENTIFICATION DIVISION." identifies a COBOL program as well as giving some brief details of its purpose.

"ENVIRONMENT DIVISION." identifies what equipment and systems are needed by a program, as well as defining where it will be run.

"SECTION." is a general purpose division. It can be used to split large programs into smaller sections, or to organize data in logical ways.

"*SOURCE." is the name of the program, as specified by the programmer.

"*CLI-SOURCE." is an optional section that contains comments to help maintain and use the program.

"*PGM-ID." is a code identifying procedural and report programs.

"DATA DIVISION.

"CONTAINS TABLES." identifies all tables that the program will process. By default, program modules are assumed to be tables.

"*ALLOCATION DETAILS.

"*ACCEPTS INPUT FROM.

"*PROMPTING FLOW-CONTROL." indicates that the program will prompt for input and provides information about how that input will be displayed to the user (such as a line number, source file, etc.).

"*ERROR-EXIT PERFORMED BY." is where error handling occurs. When one error occurs, another part of the program takes over and handles the problem.

"ENVIRONMENT DIVISION.

"INPUT-OUTPUT SECTION." contains information about files that the program reads, writes and updates.

"*FILE-CONTROL." specifies what files will be used by the program and how they are to be accessed.

"FULL-PATHNAME." references a file by its absolute path in the file system, fully qualified with a leading slash (/). The default is no leading slash.

"RELATIVE-PATHNAME.

"USING STANDARD-FILE." references a file by relative path, according to the current working directory. The default is no relative path.

"SAME-AS." indicates that the file being accessed is the same as the source file for this module (or an error or standard input). When this is specified, any lines at the beginning of a procedure that are neither "SPECIAL-NAMES" nor blank are duplicated in the output. This statement can be used to verify that the data matches in files.

"EXCLUDE." is used to exclude specific files or groups of files from an "INPUT-OUTPUT SECTION".

"RECORDING MODE IS." is used to specify whether the file being accessed is being updated.

"PERFORM MODIFICATIONS ONLY." can be specified when a file is being updated.

"ONLY." indicates that the file will only be read into memory, but not modified or output. This can be used for either sequential files or temporary storage for tables.

"READ-INTO." indicates that the file being accessed will be read into memory and no modifications will be made to it.

"*DIRECTORY." references a directory.

"RELATIVE-FILE-PATHNAME.

"RELATIVE TO." identifies a relative path to a file. The default is no relative path.

"*X10". references an X10 input device. This can be used in conjunction with the "MODIFY INPUT FILES FROM STANDARD-INPUT".

"ASSIGNED TO.

"CONTAINS THE FOLLOWING TABLES." specifies the tables that will be processed by this module.

"*IDENTIFICATION." identifies a table within the "CONTAINS TABLES". The default is zero and no such section exists.

"*NUMERIC-PRECISION." indicates that the specified table is an exact I/O port number and not a variable reference or file name.

The "FORTRAN 77 PROGRAM-ID. NAME." is the name of the program. It is used to identify programs in external files and in diagnostic messages.

"IDENTIFICATION DIVISION." identifies a FORTRAN program as well as giving some brief details of its purpose.

"ENVIRONMENT DIVISION." identifies what equipment and systems are needed by a program, as well as defining where it will be run.

"SECTION." is a general purpose division. It can be used to split large programs into smaller sections, or to organize data in logical ways.

"*DEVELOPMENT." contains programmer comments about the program.

"MODULE." is a subroutine or program unit. A module holds code that can be accessed from other parts of the program. Program modules may have parameters that must be passed and results that are returned. "MODULE-ID. NAME" is the name of the module.

"*SOURCE." is the source file name.

"*X10". references an X10 input device. This can be used in conjunction with the "MODIFY INPUT FILES FROM STANDARD-INPUT".

"*MODIFY INPUT FILES FROM STANDARD-INPUT." is written to a standard-input device and causes user input to be processed as if it were read from a long file in a sequential manner, not as character strings.

"RECORDING MODE IS." is used to specify whether the file being accessed is being updated.

"ONLY." indicates that the file will only be read into memory, but not modified or output. This can be used for either sequential files or temporary storage for tables.

"MODIFY OUTPUT FILES FROM STANDARD-OUTPUT." writes to a standard-output device and causes program output to be processed as if it were written to a sequential file, not as character strings.

"SIZES." contains parameters for a subroutine.

"GT." is less than or equal to (greater than or equal to).

"LT." is less than.

"EQV." is equivalent.

"LE." is less than or equal.

"NE." is not equal to.

"GE." is greater than or equal to (less than or equal to).

"LTE." is less than and not equal to.

"AND." is inclusive and.

"OR." is exclusive or.

"XOR." is exclusive-or.

"AGGREGATE." is a general purpose operator (like SUM, PRODUCT, MAXIMUM, etc.).

"ACCEPT INPUT FROM." defines where program input will come from. It can be either a file or a standard-input device (such as the keyboard). This can be used in conjunction with "MODIFY INPUT FILES FROM STANDARD-INPUT".

"ACCEPT OUTPUT TO." defines where program output will be sent. It can be either a file or a standard-output device (such as the screen). This can be used in conjunction with "MODIFY OUTPUT FILES FROM STANDARD-OUTPUT".

"SELECT." is used for selecting records from a file, such as a sequential file or an index. It is also used to select lines from files that are referred to by another file, such as an address file that refers to other files.

"INPUT-RECORDING MODE." is the mode used when input records are to be recorded into a file. It can be either "STATIC". This is used to create a sequential file from external commands, or "SPOOL". This is used for printing a list at the terminal.

"OUTPUT-RECORDING MODE." is the mode used when output records are to be sent to a file. It can be either "STATIC" or "SPOOL".

"INPUT SUBROUTINE." This is a subroutine that can be called by the "MODIFY INPUT FILES FROM STANDARD-INPUT". It is specified when input is to be read into a file. The TOPS-20 system does not allow subroutines to be declared in an input routine. Instead, it lets you place your code in special files referred to as control-definitions (called "DDEFs").

"OUTPUT SUBROUTINE.

"INPUT-OUTPUT SUBROUTINE." This is a subroutine that can be called by the "MODIFY INPUT FILES FROM STANDARD-INPUT" and the "MODIFY OUTPUT FILES FROM STANDARD-OUTPUT". It can also be called as an input or output subroutine by files declared in a "SECTION COMMON". The TOPS-20 system does not allow subroutines to be declared in an input or output routine. Instead, it lets you place your code in special files referred to as control-definitions (called "DDEFs").

"PROGRAM-NAME." The name of the program.

"MODULE-ID." A unique identifier of the module.

"PROGRAM-NAME." The name of the program.

"FUNCTIONAL-DOMAIN-" This string is used as a label when modules reference other modules by name. e.g. "MODULE-ID. NAME".

Chapter 7

Conditionals

Conditionals are not supported by COBOL.

COBOL supports several different kinds of conditionals:

This is practically identical to the if statement in BASIC and the equivalent construct in Visual Basic. However, since it uses a variable reference rather than a value, it can be used with any data type; for example:

This particular data type is not supported by Visual COBOL.

Multiple-statement IF statements may be used in COBOL to test conditions. A single statement following an IF statement is a separate statement and is executed only if the expression evaluating to true, as opposed to executing a number of statements inside and after the IF as described below.

The following statements are executed only if the expression evaluates to true:

IF... THEN... ELSE... END IF creates a block which executes one or more statements depending on whether or not the specified expression evaluates to true. IF... THEN can also be used as if it were a single statement, but it is called an expression instead of a statement.

An ELSE IF doesn't execute the specified statement, but rather executes the statements below it if the condition evaluates to false. In this case, each statement is executed exactly once. If there are multiple ELSE IF statements, they are executed one after another from top to bottom in the order that they appear in the code.

End-of-sentence IF statements test for a specific data type. In this case, there is no separate statement following the condition value; it is instead a set of actions. Statement execution happens only if the expression evaluating to true:

The ELSE... END IF construct can also be used to test an expression against a specific data type.

The statements inside an IF... END IF block are executed in order from top to bottom if the condition evaluates to true. This can be combined with ELSE... END IF for several conditions in one block:

In the following example, the statements foo1 and main() are executed (only if x evaluates to false) and only if foo2 is present and not null.

The IF... THEN...ELSE...END IF block is only for single statements.

The COBOL system-defined functions support conditional execution with the WHEN expression. A WHEN expression must always evaluate to TRUE or FALSE, but it may be used as a test condition for the WHEN statement.

The WHEN...THEN statement structure is identical to the IF...THEN...END IF structure.

Like BASIC and Visual Basic, COBOL has a CASE...END CASE statement for choosing among options. The syntax for a CASE statement is:

The following set of statements is executed if the expression evaluates to true:

case when "foo" then bar_action when "bar" then bar_action when others then bar_action end case

Execution ends after the first matching condition is found. The first match may be case-insensitive.

For example, the following:

causes bar_action to be executed regardless of the case of the variable.

The "whole CASE" example above is equivalent to:

The CASE...END CASE statement evaluates expressions one at a time and stops when the last expression evaluates to true, or until there are no more expressions in the CASE block. The entire block containing all cases is compiled into machine code as a single statement block, and then executed from top to bottom.

Like BASIC and Visual Basic, the exit statement is used to leave CASE blocks. It transfers program control to the next line after the entire CASE block.

COBOL also has an extended version of CASE: multiple WHEN clauses:

The actions list can contain just one action or it can contain any number of actions separated by commas. The WHEN clause with the first true expression is executed, and only that action list is executed. This is not to be confused with the 1=1 clause for TRUE, which is a part of equality expression.

The THEN clause can specify an action list as a default case. This is similar to the WHEN...THEN...ELSE statement in Visual Basic. The actions are executed if no other expression evaluates to true.

The empty WHEN clause is similar to a FALSE expression. It causes the THEN clause to be executed no matter what.

The following basic IF...THEN...ELSE statement doesn't test for null:

In the example above, only when other(x) evaluates to null does foo2() get executed. If there is an ELSE clause in the IF, then when x is not null, both foo1 and foo2() are executed.

In the same way as in Visual Basic, when the DO...END DO block is executed, the next line being executed is decremented. The same statement causes a single value to be returned to the calling code. Therefore, it is common practice to separate the code inside a DO loop with the END DO statement:

The ELSE clause can also be used with a DO...END DO loop:

This causes just one action list to be executed (the THEN clause), even if there are more actions of that action list.

A DO...END statement block can be executed multiple times:

This is similar to the FOR...STEP...NEXT structure in Visual Basic (see Control structures#For loop).

The following structured IF block doesn't check for null:

In this example above, a condition is tested at the beginning of the structured IF block, and if no condition evaluates to true, all remaining statements are skipped. This is similar to the ELSE block in Visual Basic.

This section lists commonly-used keywords.

COBOL also has a large collection of reserved words, which are used in standardized yet non-standard ways; that is, they are "reserved" to be used in specific ways by the developers, and COBOL standard does not define their implementation.

This section lists examples of various keywords being used in COBOL programming. The keywords give different names to the very same things. For example, you will find several mentions of "END-OF-FILE", instead of "END OF FILE".

As with Visual Basic, COBOL has a large suite of well-known functions. Some of these are described below.

The COBOL-defined functions are described in the COBOL 1985 standard and the current ANS X3.23:2012 standard. These are some of the most common functions used in COBOL programming:

Other built-in functions include:

A sample return format might be codice_2 which returns "The sum is" followed by the value of codice_3, then by a carriage return, and then by a line feed.

Some of these functions will not work in an interactive session, where the user is expected to type in text that is submitted over the terminal as a part of a transaction. For example, codice_4 would not work here because it expects input to be typed at the keyboard and not be directly given by the user.

Rational Rose, a model-based development environment and UML CASE tool, provides support for COBOL development.

Besides Rational Rose and other modeling tools that support the use of non-UML models for business analysis, COBOL is also supported by various CASE tools for industries such as finance.

For instance, Aprio is a cloud-based enterprise software platform that supports the design and development of business applications in either Java or COBOL.

Some companies provide additional levels of support for COBOL development, such as hosting COBOL applications in a cloud environment. For example, Intelenet offers the COBOL Builder service, a next-generation platform for application integration and deployment.

Chapter 8

Loops and Structured File Processing

What Are Loops?

A loop is a piece of code that will be executed over and over again, sometimes with some change to its condition. Usually, what's changing is the next condition in the while-statement.

Examples of loops are for loops, do while loops, and while/do/until loops. You can also use break statements to exit out of the loop when certain conditions are met. Sometimes you need an iterator variable which you increment with each iteration of the loop (eg: i=1;).

What Is Structured File Processing?

Structured file processing or data processing is a technique that uses programs to populate and update databases as well as handle reports. There are a number of techniques that are used to manage the data. Structured file processing is not a well-recognized terminology, but it's described in IBM's COBOL for MVS/ESA V4R4 Programmer's Reference and illustrated in many textbooks and articles on COBOL programming.

What Is Cobol Script?

Cobol Script is a programming language that is derived from COBOL which enhances its functionality by adding objects, polymorphism and object-oriented constructs. It uses English words instead of technical words so it's easier to read and understand unlike traditional COBOL that was more machine oriented. It allows the programmer to be more productive and understand their code better. It provides easier access to Enterprise Data and help unite business people and IT professionals by using familiar English language terms instead of the strict programming syntax of COBOL.

COBOL is still very popular for a reason, it's a standard programming language that has been around for over 50 years now. It's main strength is its stability, it can still be used to write new applications without needing to learn a new programming language like Java or C++ because it can run on any computer but you may need to run an older version of Java on your computer to make it compatible with older COBOL programs. A lot of software is still written in COBOL because it's one of the few programming languages that can be used to create applications for mainframes. It's a good language to learn as it will give you a good foundation for learning other programming languages.

Why Use Cobol?

Cobol is designed for business-centric applications, and particularly for applications that must maintain their integrity over long periods of time. Programmers using Cobol can write applications that are generally easier to understand than in other languages such as C++ or Java.

What Is 'Cobol Samples'?

There are many companies and websites that are offering free Cobol software or tutorials. You can find large amount of Cobol software on the internet but many of them are outdated or not working. Cobol-samples.ca offers free workable and up to date samples that you can use to run and test your own code in a sample environment. The samples include file processing, string processing, all the classic commands that are used in daily programming and also special sections like file testing, parse statements, REXX samples, operating system calls and more.

The main idea behind this website is to provide free samples for COBOL programmers that they can use easily as a starting point for their own coding. It doesn't matter whether you've never programmed before or want to learn COBOL using the most up-to-date samples. Cobol-samples.ca strives to be as user friendly as possible so that no one will feel intimidated by the language and can easily understand it even if they have never previously discussed COBOL before.

IBM processors first came on the market in 1959; the IBM 7000 series of computers was a step towards programmability in business operation by making programs extendable and efficient. In 1964, the UNIVAC 1108 was introduced to provide security for data entry into mainframe computers. This move towards secure data processing and programmability, provided the opportunity for COBOL to be introduced into the mainframe computer business.

In 1959, business applications were first introduced to the operating system. A programmer named Grace Hopper rented a machine from IBM and created the first compiler in 1960. This event is often referred to as "the giant step," and her work was later named FLOW-MATIC. Advancements in technology have made computers faster and more powerful since then. Now, programmers can create systems that are larger, more complex, and more powerful than ever before imagined with COBOL.

COBOL was the first programming language that had a standard to adhere to when creating code. It was important for businesses because programs could be created to work across various platforms and manufacturers, making them more powerful and efficient. Using COBOL as a programming language has proven its worth throughout the years, and continues to be used by organizations around the globe.

All COBOL statements, for example read, write, and search statements, contain LOOP statements. The loop control structure allows a program to perform the same task over and over until certain conditions are met. The repetition is outlined by the programmer in three steps:

Programmers can use loops to process on a record-by-record basis. Some of the most notable uses of this feature include inventory control processing and banking operations. But it is easy to see that COBOL's support for structured file processing could be applied to a wide array of situations.

The COBOL statement to process on a record-by-record basis is the PERFORM verb. PERFORM can be used in two ways, either as an ordinary or extended verb:

Programmers should note that the WHEN phrase is optional in an extended PERFORM statement. If WHEN is omitted, it defaults to DO UNTIL. In some implementations of COBOL, it is possible to omit the WHERE clause as well, which defaults the END-PERFORM statement to DO WHILE.

PERFORM can be used for more than just reading data from a file into a program and processing it one record at a time. It can also be used to store data into a file. For example, if you wanted to write all the data in a table into a file, the PERFORM statement could be used as follows:

In COBOL PERFORM is not the only way to write out data. You can also use the WITHDRAW verb. However, this may not be useful in instances where multiple programs process the same data and want to share that information. A good example of this is when two programs process a job file or some other data source, and you wish to keep track of that information between runs.

COBOL handles structured file processing by using a series of data-transferring verbs. These are the READ, WRITE, INQUIRE, and REWRITE verbs. The INQUIRE verb is used to get data from a file or report. It is important to note that this verb can only be used for display purposes and not for program input. It is possible however to use it to get information from the program output screen into your program.

Readers of COBOL should be careful when using the INQUIRE verb, because it could lead to a security breach if the data is not handled correctly. The following example shows a very basic use of the INQUIRE verb:

The most common use of the INQUIRE verb is to get data from the data source. In this case, you do not need to use explicit program control statements such as DO or IF. Just put the contents of each record into your program one at a time:

This technique, however, does have its limitations. It is not possible to use the INQUIRE statement to pull data into the program if you are performing a search and replace operation. You can, however, use the READ verb to get a current value from the screen at any given time:

These two examples show that COBOL supports complex operations. It is not just limited to reading data from the file. You can also modify your program by using some of these verbs. This means that you could write a program to edit or delete data from a file.

COBOL also provides a way for programmers to write temporary data into a file. This is accomplished using the REWRITE verb. With the REWRITE verb you can replace data in a file that may have been updated with the same or different data. The following instructions will show you how to use this function to change one record in an existing file:

A very common use of the READ, WRITE and INQUIRE/REWRITE verbs is for creating report or summary lists of information. These reports are commonly used for reporting purposes by management and by users.

The INQUIRE or REWRITE verb can also be used for character string processing. It is possible to get the length of a string, get certain characters from it, and even add characters. For example, the following instructions show you how to get the length of a string:

COBOL has support for character field processing. This is supported by the "MOVE" verb. This verb takes up to three arguments; data source, field location and field length. For example, this move statement could be used to update two fields in your program:

A common practice when writing input programs is to use an edit mask. An example of this would be to say, "If the value of the field is all blank, then set the field to 'employee'".

The problem with this method is that it creates a lot of complexity for your program. It can also be disadvantageous because you are not always sure what information you may want to exclude. The following example shows how this can be solved:

In COBOL there are no restrictions on edit masks. You could include one in your program that looks like this: This "mask" will always return "employee" no matter what you put into the other two fields. Since it uses REWRITE, this mask would also change any values associated with the object being processed.

COBOL programs are processed in sequence without branching; that is, a COBOL program only performs one action (one step) at a time unless it needs to recalculate data for execution. For instance, if an assignment was not found for an employee who wants a raise and who might be promoted then no action will be taken. However, if there are enough tasks left in the day then this particular employee can get their raise and promotion when they have time to complete them all on time.

Chapter 9

Error Handling and Exceptions

COMMON ERROR TRAP MEANINGS AND CORRECTIONS

1. FILE I/O error 202: Unable to open file "filename". This means the hard drive containing the filename in question is not allocated or not available. Delete all files in that directory and try again.

2. FILE I/O error 203: Unable to close file "filename". This means that the system cannot close this particular file window, or access to it is denied by some other software program. Look at the security

tab of this window, and see if there is anything else preventing you from closing the window properly (for example, someone may have locked your computer).

3. FILE I/O error 204: Unable to write into file "filename". This means your file is locked and the program which created it locked it before you even tried to write into it. Unlock this file and try again.

4. FILE I/O error 205: Unable to read from file "filename". This means your file is unlocked, but has a password set on it. (Or, once again, someone has locked this file and blocked you from accessing it.) Either unlock the file or ask for the person who locked it to unlock the computer for you.

5. FILE I/O error 206: Unable to flush output file buffer. This means that, for some unknown reason, the computer cannot clear its RAM buffer and therefore write to the disk. Step 1: Press Ctrl+Alt+Delete on your keyboard. This will open the Windows Task Manager window. Click on the "Performance" tab at the top of this window and click on "Disk". Then click on the disk drive named "C:" (usually this is your hard drive). This will open up a window which shows how much space you have left on your hard drive (the top number) and how much total memory you have used (the bottom number). If you don't see any information here about your hard-drive, consult Step 2 below.

Step 2: To fix this problem, open up the "Administrative Tools" window. This is a window that you can access by clicking on "Start" then "All Programs". You should see a system window here called "Administrative Tools". Click once on this (if you don't see it, click on "Start" again to go back from here and you will be able to find it). There should now be a window which looks similar to this:

From here, click on the arrow in the top left corner of your screen (this icon is usually just called '-' and sometimes has a square around it). Now select the option that says 'Advanced System Settings'. If you don't see this option, then click on "Start" again and choose "Control Panel" this time.

A new window should appear:

From here, click once on the "System Configuration" tab. There should be a window now like this one:

At the bottom of the screen, you will see a drop-down menu called "Advanced". Click on this. Now find the section which says "Performance Options". This is where you need to go if you are having problems with your computer. Also make sure to check the box which says 'Debugging Tools'.

Apply these changes and then click OK to save them.

Step 3: To fix this problem, restart your computer. If that doesn't work, put the computer into 'Safe Mode'. To do this, turn your computer on and as soon as you see the BIOS screen (where you press F2 or F12 or whatever key is right for your specific computer), immediately press the 'F8' key. This will open up another menu. Look through this menu until you find a menu option which says something like "Safe Mode with Networking" or "Start Windows Normally". Press whichever key it tells you to use to open that option and it will save your computer in 'Safe Mode'.

Step 4: To fix this problem, restart your computer and/or remove the device you are trying to access. Restart your computer and try again. This is usually a USB drive, so take the USB drive out and try again.

5. FILE I/O error 401: Unable to open file "filename". This means that someone else has locked a file on your computer and you cannot access it. Usually this means you either did not give permission for that particular person to access that particular file or you only have permission for them to do so if the file is locked (i.e., if it has a password).

6. Unknown COBOL class message. This means there is a new version of COBOL which has not been translated, or the translation is not complete. There are two versions of COBOL (original, and modern). Original COBOL has been translated into around 100 languages, but modern COBOL requires over 800 languages to be translated. Kindly contact your local translator to see if they are able to translate the relevant phrases into your language.

7. File IO error 202: Unable to open file "filename". This means you have a file which you cannot open because it is locked or password protected (or both). To unlock this particular file, right-click on the file and select 'Properties' from the menu that appears.

Make sure that the 'Read-Only' option is NOT selected. You can make this file locked again if you want to by selecting the 'Read-Only' option.

If you cannot see the 'Properties' menu, then it is probably because you do not have permission to access this file. In which case, you should ask whoever owns it to unlock it for you.

8. FILE I/O error 203: Unable to close file "filename". This means that a file has been closed which you are still trying to access. Either the person who opened that file closed it before you had finished accessing it or another program has managed to open and close the same file before you had finished writing to it. Make sure the application which opened this file is not running and try again.

9. FILE I/O error 202: Unable to write into file "filename". (You might also see FILE I/O error 201: Unable to read from file "filename". Usually this is due to a temporary problem, but if the error message repeats itself very often, it might be due to something more serious.) This means there is something wrong with your computer's hard drive. This can be a problem with the actual hard drive itself or the software you are using (such as Norton Antivirus).

10. FILE I/O error 304: Unable to create stream on filename. This means that you are trying to run a program which requires a file which no longer exists. If this is happening a lot, then you should contact your anti-virus software provider and see if they can restore your files for you.

11. 404 Machine Format Error: This error message is displayed if your computer tries to access an Internet page but cannot find it. You need to check that the web address (URL) is correct or try the related links below this article for help with finding it.

12. 404 Page Not Found: This error is displayed when you try to open a web page which no longer exists. This message often appears if the web address (URL) you are using is incorrect or out of date. You need to check that the web address (URL) is correct or try the related links below this article for help with finding it.

13. 404 Document Not Found: This error message may appear if you are trying to access a document or picture on an old Windows NT 4.0 computer (which does not have ActiveX scripts enabled). To fix this problem, right-click on the file in question and select 'Save As'. Now right-click and select 'Save' to save the file in the relevant folder and then right-click on the file again, but this time select 'Open' rather than 'Save'. You should also see a menu which allows you to 'Run'. Click on that menu and find the program which says "Internet Explorer". Select it, and then let it run. The problem should be solved.

Data Manipulation Features

Cobol has data manipulation features similar to other programming languages.

Data can be sorted, searched, and copied. COBOL has the following operations:

General file copying

Sort files by date or numeric field

Search files when keyword is in data

Data manipulation operators are used in expressions for these data manipulations operations. The operands in an expression are evaluated from left to right with all operations being executed before any result is returned. The order of evaluation does not change the meaning of the expression but execution sequence may be significant in some cases.

Features like COBOL RETURN, are handy for formatting data. But when errors occur in these COBOL programs, it's up to the programmer to handle them. The most common error types in COBOL programs are exceptions and errors that occur during file handling operations.

The basic syntax for the RETURN statement in COBOL is:

In cases where there are no exception in the program, the program will return to the READ or DISPLAY statement.

For exception handling COBOL has an error-class scheme. There are six error classes with a couple of exceptions and most exceptions are grouped into one of these classes.

Error-class scheme for COBOL

The error class is a major factor in how errors are handled in COBOL. It's a good idea to handle as many exceptions as possible early on in the program. The RETURN statement is very handy for formatting data when there are no errors but when there are, the programmer has to handle problems.

Programmers can take steps to prevent these problems by using stack-based operation code and proper exception handlers.

Table-driven, program-calling features

It was designed to address the business data processing needs of small to large computer users. COBOL is a compiled language that has extended, structured facilities for data manipulation and relative ease of learning. COBOL is a generation language that supports later type checking and more sophisticated runtimes, but it lacks the generality needed for some applications.

In today's computerized office environment, COBOL is generally used to handle the basic data entry and data transfer operations. In smaller organizations, COBOL may be the only programming language used. The machine-code instruction set built into machines prior to the introduction of assembly languages like C is limited by word size usually 32 bits in size. For example, a string operation may require an operation code consisting of 28 bits (1 byte).

To address these limitations, a machine-language instruction set developed by IBM for its 1620 computer. Machines with this instruction set include the 360, 1400, and 7090. The instruction set features 32-bit words—an extended data word—and 64-bit registers. In addition, interrupts are available to handle external events such as keyboard entry and output.

Machine-coded COBOL programs can be translated or tokenized into low-level machine language using a compiler or interpreter with great flexibility. After translation, the program can be directly embedded into memory, or written to disk or punched cards.

COBOL has been described as only a translator between high-level languages and lower level machine instructions. This is incorrect. COBOL often uses a number of subroutines that contain statements from these lower-level languages like machine code, ALGOL 60 and PL/I that are called "assembler subroutines" by some text books.

The main reason for the central location of COBOL as an instruction set language is that it provides high level constructs like data manipulation, cross-referencing variables, COBOL record structures and file handling.

COBOL can be used to write programs in other languages. However, a COBOL program will not likely run well on the same platform with the other language. Programming languages like Fortran, BASIC and PASCAL are good examples of high-level languages. COBOL is similar to a language like Fortran. However, the differences between COBOL and Fortran are more significant than the similarities.

The features of COBOL include:

Relative ease of learning

Programmers can be productive in a short time period with the structured facilities for data manipulation and table-driven, program-calling features like other generation programming languages. There is a lot of variety in COBOL programming with the different exceptions and features.

Programmers who have used languages like C and Fortran have found it not difficult to learn COBOL.

COBOL is an English-like language, so it has a natural feel that many programmers say they do not find in other languages. This ease of learning is convenience for the programmer, but can be an issue when changes occur to the program.

COBOL is widely used in small to large sized organizations and is popular among programmers that have experience in other languages.

The machine-code instruction set built into machines prior to the introduction of assembly languages like C is limited by word size usually 32 bits in size. For example, a string operation may require an operation code consisting of 28 bits (1 byte). To address these limitations, a machine-language instruction set developed by IBM for its 1620 computer. Machines with this instruction set include the 360, 1400, and 7090. The instruction set features 32-bit words—an extended data word—and 64-bit registers. In addition, interrupts are available to handle external events such as keyboard entry and output. Machine-coded COBOL programs can be translated or tokenized into low-level machine language using a compiler or interpreter with great flexibility. After translation, the program can be directly embedded into memory, or written to disk or punched cards.

COBOL has been described as only a translator between high-level languages and lower level machine instructions. This is incorrect. COBOL often uses a number of subroutines that contain statements from these lower-level languages like machine code, ALGOL 60 and PL/I that are called "assembler subroutines" by some text books.

The data type structure in COBOL is based on the Data Description Framework (DDL). The programmer has to follow a specific format to write the program. There are 37 data types in COBOL based on the DDL. Some of these data types include:

The programmer must use a combination of keywords and lengths to indicate the format or length of each field. For example, "codice_1" indicates an alphanumeric field that can be up to 30 characters long with no leading zeros. When writing COBOL statements, they must maintain three sets in order: Alphabetic, numeric and special characters. The special characters that must be included in COBOL statements are: +-*/=, ( ), < > and blank. COBOL allows you to use the wild card character * to match any number of any character, whereas SQL does not allow this.

The main types of data manipulation in COBOL include input and output, file manipulations and table manipulation. Data

Input/Output (I/O) can be accomplished by reading data from files or devices or by writing it to a file or device. The "codice_2" and "codice_3" clauses are used to read, write and output data. File manipulation features of COBOL include codice_4, codice_5, codice_6 and codice_7. These features allow the programmer to set up files and the way they are handled. Table manipulation is accomplished using the different table operators: index-by tables, relative and direct address tables, sorted tables and table insertions.

Data types can be differentiated based on their sizes and whether they are used in fixed or varying length fields. In COBOL, there are three types of data: fix format, variable format and free format.

Variables come with different data types and can be classified as elementary types, composite types and special type. Elementary type variables have simple structures that do not include other structures. Composite variables contain various structures within them such as elementary variables. Special type includes global variables, parameters and fields.

COBOL variables are initialized using the codice_8 keyword and must be declared by the programmer. The codice_9 specifies that a variable is one of many similar variables within a source line. Variables can be defined as constant, display and record formats. COBOL constants are fixed values that do not change throughout the program, whereas display formats are fixed formats that can change with certain entries.

There are two types of variables: external and internal. External variables must be declared with specific qualifiers (codice_10), whereas internal variables do not need qualifiers because they can be accessed directly within the program. Intermediary variables are the intermediate or temporary variables that are passed between procedures.

Data can be stored into variables using codice_11 data type operators. Variables are specified as "codice_12" for numeric, "codice_13" for alphanumeric and "codice_14" for character data types. Data types like codice_15, codice_16 and codice_17 have been eliminated from COBOL versions later than version 7.

COBOL allows programs to be written in text files, which can be read and modified by users or other applications. In COBOL, the programmer must use a specific format when writing a procedure in order to keep up with the internal processing of COBOL. The layout of these procedures is called the "COBOL Copybook". There are three types of entries that are used in the COBOL Copybook. These entries are:

The first two data types include a description, which is usually a brief description of the procedure. A COBOL procedure can contain more than one source line, but each source line must have a unique name. Source lines must be terminated with a semi-colon and terminated by the following statement: codice_19. The codice_20 keyword is used to read the input data stored in a file. The codice_21 keyword is used to output the program results on a file.

There is no limit to the number of procedures in a COBOL program, but each procedure must have a unique name. Procedures can be called using the codice_22 keyword and return results using the codice_23 statement.

Source code can be written in text files by using the Code writing conventions in COBOL. Text editing and execution of the program can be accomplished using the "codice_24" line. Other commands that may be included in a text file are as follows:

This statement is used to read the input data stored in a file called codice_25. The first part of this statement (codice_26) indicates that the procedure is accessing an input file. The second part (codice_27) indicates that the procedure is reading from a source line. The third part (codice_28) indicates that the procedure is reading from the codice_25 file.

The file used to store the program's results is called codice_29 and must have a unique name in order to access it by using this statement. The first part (codice_30) indicates that the procedure is accessing a data file. The second part (codice_31) a variable called "name" which is used to distinguish between different output files. The third part (codice_28) is used to indicate the name of the file.

This statement is used to output the program results on a file called codice_25. The first part of this statement (codice_26) indicates that the procedure is accessing an output file. The second part (codice_27) indicates that the procedure is writing to a source line.

The third part (codice_28) indicates that the procedure is writing to the codice_25 file.

Many other statements are available for text file manipulation, but are not listed in the above table because they are generally used for concatenation and comment purposes. There are also other statements that can be used such as codice_35 and codice_36.

codice_37 is a statement used when a COBOL program is being defined by a programmer or developer . This statement instructs COBOL that the procedure being created is ready to be defined into the copybook for use.

codice_38 is a statement that defines the source lines that are used within a procedure. These source lines can be included in the copybook.

codice_39 is used to conditionally branch from one procedure to another procedure or from one part of the program to another part of the program based on a certain criteria. The following table indicates the types of codice_40 statements and how they are used:

codice_41 is also known as an "IF-THEN" statement. This statement is used to tell COBOL to branch forward to the second part of the program if the first part of this statement is true.

codice_42 is a statement that tells COBOL to execute a certain piece of code based on whether or not the conditions are met. These statements are made up of one or more conditions connected by an operator, as seen in the following table:

codice_44 is also known as an "END IF" statement. These statements are used to tell COBOL to exit the codice_40 statement.

codice_46 is used to branch to another program or procedure.

codice_47 is the "ELSE" part of the codice_49 statement. This statement is used to tell COBOL that if a certain condition fails, then do something else. The "ELSE" part mostly works with an IF-THEN condition, but can work with other conditions as well .

codice_50 is used to give a specific value to a variable. These statements are made up of one or more conditions connected by an operator, as seen in the following table:

codice_52 is the "END IF" part of the codice_49 statement. This statement is used to tell COBOL that if a certain condition fails, then do not do something else. The "END IF" part mostly works with an IF-THEN condition, but can work with other conditions as well .

COBOL allows a statement to be formatted using different styles, but allows only one style per program.

Chapter 10

Text IO, Dates, and Times
(Time Processing)

The COBOL language has a powerful set of built-in capabilities when it comes to text processing, dates and times. In this section we'll be looking at the logic for these three topics: text IO, dates and times, and exceptions.

Text Input functions in COBOL are built around the INPUT statement. We will look at how different text inputs are handled in greater detail later on. For now we can just think of two ways to handle input, using the INPUT statement or processing the user's character input through a direct read function.

The INPUT statement uses the format, keyword and variable to input a string. Each of these keywords is given its own function within COBOL. The format will be shown in a moment, but for now we'll look at the variable keyword.

Note that either of these methods may be used to read from a file or from an already assembled statement line. They are just two different ways of doing the same thing. The mechanism is not important, just that they can do the job they were intended to do.

For this example we will use format (1) as shown below. We'll examine the other formats later on in each topic.

The INPUT statement has a format (1) and the format parameter is set to the number of characters to be input from the user, starting in column 0s. The rest of the parameters are set by default for you, but can be modified if you want.

Note that there are many more parameters available for what to alert you about when an input function fails.

When the INPUT statement cannot process a string of text, it will return a value and set an error bit to ON. The following example shows how to test for this condition by using the END-IF statement:

Note that there is no other COBOL code for this example. All of the processing is done in the INPUT and END-IF statements. The failure is only detected when the INPUT function returns with an error value.

The following shows an example of another format for INPUT (2).

As in the first example, this one is to be expected since there is no parameter to read from the user. The PICTURE statement will return with a value of zero (0) if there were any pictures that were input.

There are many other formats for INPUT (1) and (2), so we'll look at them next. Note that you can use different formats within the same program, but each must have its own set of parameters for the specific INPUT function.

In most modern versions of COBOL, you do not need a separate FOR loop to read a number range into one or more variables. Instead, it can be done with a DATA step.

The following is a simple example to read ten (10) characters one at a time from the user:

After the first statement is executed, all variables that are assigned in the "DATA DIVISION" will be set to empty. So you must execute the second statement prior to reading any of the data into these variables.

The user is prompted for input and must enter ten (10) characters, one (1) character per line. The program will report what was entered and assign it accordingly. The program then prompts for another set of ten (10) values. For each prompt and input, the previous data will be overwritten by subsequent value sets.

You can also shorten the program by doing away with the printing of prompts. The following is another example without prompts being printed.

Note that you must use two asterisks to terminate a DATA line.

Note that this method will read data only in columns 0 through 9, as specified by the indicator values at lines 13 and 14. Indicators are special values used in COBOL to control program execution, by setting variables and/or testing conditions. They are stored in a table called the indicator table ( ) at column 17 of each line (record) of an area on disk called "Control Break" or just "Control".

The status of indicators will affect any processing done in the current or subsequent lines. Thus, the indicator present on line 14 at that time will determine whether an IF statement is executed, or a DATA step will be executed.

In addition to the indicator on line 14 (column 17), you can have various indicators in Control Break 12 through 20 (columns 9 through 14). It is a good idea to recognize those indicators and what they mean.

The indicator to get input from the user is called INPUT-ERR. This value is set to 1 when an input string cannot be processed because of insufficient length, invalid format, etc. The default value of this indicator is zero (0), and it is left to the programmer to set it to 1 if the INPUT or INSPECT functions encounter an error during execution. The IF-THEN-ELSE statement can be used to test the INPUT-ERR indicator at lines 17 through 19.

Note that you must use two asterisks to terminate a DATA line.

Note that this method will read data only in columns 0 through 9, as specified by the indicator values at lines 13 and 14. Indicators are special values used in COBOL to control program execution, by setting variables and/or testing conditions. They are stored in a table called the indicator table ( ) at column 17 of each line (record) of an area on disk called "Control Break" or just "Control".

The status of indicators will affect any processing done in the current or subsequent lines. Thus, the indicator present on line 14 at that time will determine whether an IF statement is executed, or a DATA step will be executed. In addition to the indicator on line 14 (column 17), you can have various indicators in Control Break 12 through 20 (columns 9 through 14). It is a good idea to recognize those indicators and what they mean. For example, INPUT-ERR means that there was some kind of error during input.

The following shows a more complex example that uses the INPUT-ERR indicator to detect a situation where no input was entered from the user:

Note that there is no printout of text prompts because this version would not be useful if there were any number of prompts. The only purpose for printing out the text prompts is to show what was set in response to each prompt. When you see some text that you cannot make sense of, or cannot imagine why any attempt at an input failed, then take a look at these control lines and think about whether they indicate anything like what you might expect a valid input to do.

Note also that there are some really silly things that can happen on line 13 of an area. For example, when you run the source code above, on your screen you will see the following:

RAB = "Invalid Format" YLN = "Invalid Characters" PSC = "Insufficient Arguments" SOY = "Specified Only Y (No L or N)" SHO = "Specified Only X (No O or M)" STARS = "Specified Only a Number in a Number Separator" PRI-NUMBER-NO-DOUBLE-SPACE = "Unprintable Character Sequence".

There is more than one way to read user data. You can get user input with an interactive program called a Job Control Language (JCL) used to execute user programs on a mainframe, or you can read from a file using the MERGE statement.

The program above is simple enough for us to examine it in more detail. The second statement prints out the text prompt. In COBOL, print statements can be used without any programming logic in them. They are called "executable print statements" and do not require any executable code to run them.

The third statement reads data from the user and assigns it to two variables, "RAB" and "YLN". There are two forms of the INPUT function available: (1) and (2). The first reads up to a specified number of characters, while the second reads an entire line or record and assigns it to one or more variables.

The difference between these two forms is that the INPUT(1) function stops reading as soon as it finds a carriage return (ASCII 13), while INPUT(2) does not stop until it reaches the end of the line or record. The third statement will continue to read input until a carriage return is entered.

If you do not use indicators in COBOL, you will have no way of determining whether any input was actually entered. So, to make valid assumptions, you have to have some way of monitoring the user's input. If you use indicators with the INPUT function, however, some control will be lost because the program has access only to columns 0 - 9, and there is no means by which you can tell what was typed into columns 10 - 80. This is not a problem if all that you need is a simple username and password but it can be if your needs are more complex.

To resolve this problem we can use an interactive program called Job Control Language (JCL) which allows us to give our COBOL programs direct access to user input by using a system command called "OPTION COPY".

Chapter 11

Data Access Methods
(Interfacing With DBMSes)

C OBOL has database access methods for interfacing with various DBMSes. Two of the most common of COBOL's DBMS interfaces are known as the "I" and "W" methods. The I interface is often called Data soft's COBOL, because this company innovated that approach back in 1983. Most programs written under this interface will use a section label beginning with an 'I' and ending with '.DB'.

The W method is known as the Workspace Interface Method, which was an innovation by Micro Focus way back in 1984. Most programs written under this interface will use a section label beginning with a 'W' and ending in '.DB'.

The I and W methods are generally referred to as "SQL" methods.

Some examples of the I and W methods are given below. Note that the section labels used here are arbitrary; they don't match those used in any of the COBOL reference manuals, and it's up to you how to interpret them.

After this introductory material, you will find more detailed explanations of how these methods get performed, with some examples and links to further information.

COBOL Index (I) method example:

Add the following lines to an empty file. Call it FILE, and place it in a set of source files that will be compiled using Micro Focus COBOL for i5/OS.

The first four lines are the DDS for the source file. For simplicity, the data will consist of only one record, and will be stored in a subset of the JOB_HISTORY table from my own test DBMS named MYDB, which can be accessed from within IBM's i5/OS or via SQL Server or Oracle on Linux or Solaris. The schema used here is compatible with other DBMSs that also use hierarchical storage models. The JOB_HISTORY table is a subset of the CANDIDATE_OBJECT table, which is a subset of OBJECT. The schema and data should be clear in this hierarchical storage model.

The first line of the control section is the label for the data division. In this example, only one record will be retrieved, so this is not a real table (record-oriented), but a pseudo table (scalar). All COBOL applications that work with hierarchical databases must define scalar tables.

The second line is called "the format specification." The format determines which pseudo fields are to be read from the DBMS and written to the screen or printed on paper. Each field can automatically be assigned an identifier in COBOL source code, which makes it possible to refer to it in future instructions via its identifier.

All of these fields are identified by their positions within the JOB_HISTORY table. Note that the format specification is used to retrieve three fields:

The last line of the control section is the cursor declaration. This tells COBOL which DBMS it will use, as well as which table (the pseudo table) and which SQL statement (the SQL statement) will be used. This line specifies that if no records were found for display or for update, a message with two columns should be displayed on the screen. The first column should contain a "non-null" character (*), and the second column a "null" character (*).

Note that this cursors declaration can be processed even if there are no records in MYDB. The program will still be executed and no message will be displayed on the screen. But if there are some records, the cursor declaration has to be altered to display an appropriate message.

COBOL Unspecified Addressing Modifier (I) method example:

Add the following lines to an empty file in a set of source files that will be compiled with Micro Focus COBOL for i5/OS. Call this file FILE, and place it in the same directory as FILE.DDS, which is in a set of source files that will be compiled under Micro Focus COBOL for i5/OS.

The control section begins with an empty line and ends with ".END". It does not perform any DBMS access. (COBOL does not require you to do this.)

In the data division, declare a pseudo table to be named "FILE-DATUM". This is a regular COBOL table that can store nulls. It will be used as the data source for some SQL statement that retrieves two fields from the JOB_HISTORY table and writes them to a screen or paper file.

The control section begins with an empty line and ends with ".END". It performs no DBMS access whatsoever, but it must be present in all COBOL programs that use SQL methods. This is the "I" control specification.

The first line of the control section is an attribute specification. This specifies that one field from the ARCHIVE_OBJECT table must be written to a file named FILE_LOG. The label for this file is unchanged from that used in the DDS for FILE.DDS. The data division will read one field from that table, and write it to the specified file.

The second line of the control section is an access specification. It tells COBOL what SQL statement should be used to read one field from ARCHIVE_OBJECT, and write it to FILE_LOG.

The first line of the control section is an empty line followed by ".APPEND". This causes the DBMS to append the field that was read from ARCHIVE_OBJECT to the file "FILE_LOG" without overwriting any data in that file.

File "FILE_LOG" gets updated with a new record once per run of this program.

COBOL Unspecified Modifier (U) method example:

Add the following lines to an empty file in a set of source files that will be compiled with Micro Focus COBOL for i5/OS. Call this file FILE, and place it in the same directory as FILE.DDS and FILE_LOG.DDS, which are in a set of source files that will be compiled under Micro Focus COBOL for i5/OS. The last 4 lines that start with an asterisk are the control section.

The second line of the control section is an empty line followed by ".APPEND". This causes the DBMS to append any fields read from ARCHIVE_OBJECT to the file "FILE_LOG" without overwriting any data in that file.

The last four lines are a cursor declaration. It indicates that if no records were found for display or update, a message with two columns should be displayed on screen and/or written to a file named FILE_LOG. The first column should contain a "non-null" character (*), and the second column a "null" character (*).

The first line of the control section is an empty line followed by ".APPEND". This indicates that the DBMS should append any fields read from ARCHIVE_OBJECT to the file name specified in the cursor declaration above.

The last four lines are a cursor declaration. It indicates that if no records were found for update or display, a message with two

115

columns should be displayed on screen and/or written to a file named FILE_LOG. The first column should contain a "non-null" character (*), and the second column a "null" character (*).

The first line of the control section is an empty line followed by ".APPEND". This indicates that the DBMS should append any fields read from ARCHIVE_OBJECT to the file name specified in the cursor declaration above.

COBOL Unspecified Modifier (U) method example:

Add the following lines to an empty file in a set of source files that will be compiled with Micro Focus COBOL for i5/OS. Call this file FILE, and place it in the same directory as FILE.DDS, which is in a set of source files that will be compiled under Micro Focus COBOL for i5/OS. The file FILE_LOG.DDS, which is in a set of source files that will be compiled under Micro Focus COBOL for i5/OS, was used to demonstrate the use of controls.

The control section begins with an empty line and ends with ".END". It does not perform any DBMS access whatsoever. (COBOL does not require you to do this.)

In the data division, declare a pseudo table to be named "FILE_OBJECT". This is a regular COBOL table that can store nulls. It will be used as the data source for some SQL statement that retrieves two fields from the JOB_HISTORY table and writes them either to a screen or paper file.

The control section begins with an empty line and ends with ".END". It performs no DBMS access whatsoever, but it must be present in all COBOL programs that use SQL methods. This is the "U" control specification.

The first line of the control section is an attribute specification. This specifies that one field from the ARCHIVE_OBJECT table must be written to a file named FILE_LOG. The label for this file is unchanged from that used in the DDS for FILE.DDS. The data division will read one field from that table, and write it to the specified file.

The second line of the control section is an access specification. It tells COBOL what SQL statement should be used to read one field from ARCHIVE_OBJECT and write it to FILE_LOG.

The first line of the control section is an empty line followed by ".APPEND". This causes the DBMS to append any field read from ARCHIVE_OBJECT to the file "FILE_LOG" without overwriting any data in that file.

File "FILE_LOG" gets updated with a new record once per run of this program.

COBOL Obsolete System (O) method example:

Add the following lines to an empty file in a set of source files that will be compiled with Micro Focus COBOL for i5/OS. Call this file FILE, and place it in the same directory as FILE.DDS and FILE_LOG.DDS, which are in a set of source files that will be compiled under Micro Focus COBOL for i5/OS. The last four lines that start with an asterisk are the control section.

The third line of the control section is an access specification. It tells COBOL what SQL statement should be used to read one field from ARCHIVE_OBJECT, and write it to FILE_LOG.

The first line of the control section is an empty line followed by ".APPEND". This indicates that the DBMS should append any field read from ARCHIVE_OBJECT to the file "FILE_LOG" without overwriting any data in that file.

File "FILE_LOG" gets updated with a new record once per run of this program.

COBOL System (S) method example:

Add the following lines to an empty file in a set of source files that will be compiled with Micro Focus COBOL for i5/OS. Call this file FILE, and place it in the same directory as FILE.DDS, which is in a set of source files that will be compiled under Micro Focus COBOL for i5/OS. The file FILE_LOG.DDS, which is in a set of source files that will be compiled under Micro Focus COBOL for i5/OS, was used to demonstrate the use of controls.

Chapter 12

Cobol Programming Utilities

C obol programming utilities were developed in the late 1950s and early 1960s - before other programming languages had even emerged. This archaic programming language is still taught in some colleges.

Cobol stands for Common Business Oriented Language. It was created by Grace Hopper, one of the Navy's first computer programmers, who also coined the term "computer bug." The initial name for Cobol was Common Business Oriented Language (COBOL).

To create Cobol programs, you must know about a wide range of programming concepts and techniques. For example, you must understand what keywords are, how to use them and the control structures. You must know how to assign values and constants. You should know how to organize data, what data types and sizes of fields would be ideal for various applications.

Cobol is the formal name of a language created by Grace Hopper in 1952 at the University of Wisconsin–Milwaukee (UWM) in collaboration with computer engineer Tom Stayman that was used on mainframe computers. About 300 Cobol programmers worked on the first core Cobol system. Cobol was the commercial version of the language. It was first implemented in 1959 on the IBM 704 computer.

COBOL's syntax is based on English. Syntax rules are like grammar rules, which tell you how to arrange words and other elements into sentences. Syntax also tells you how to arrange code statements into program statements, and how to organize those statements in a sequence that makes sense when a computer runs them.

Cobol has three types of syntax:

The actual programming process is written out in sequential order just as it would be if a human programmer were writing a program; however, the program logic might be executed by machine instead of human beings. The program is divided into sections and sub sections which are further subdivided. Code written in Cobol is also called source code.

Scope of variables in COBOL:

COBOL offers several ways to use variables. Variables, or identifiers, are used to store data or retrieve data from a storage location. The term identifier was chosen because it represents something that can be "identified" (i.e., pointed out). In COBOL identifiers are used to represent the names of variables and constants. Identifiers can be up to 10 characters long and can contain letters from the English alphabet and numbers. An identifier's first character must be a letter from the English alphabet (or an underscore). Identifiers are case-sensitive. They may or may not include underscores. The underscore is commonly used in programming to improve the readability of code.

This example below shows a simple COBOL program that takes two numbers as input, adds them together and displays the sum on screen:

```
5 IF X + Y GTR 10 THEN STOP RUN
```

In this example, the file is called DISPLAY.CBL and it contains:

```
IDENTIFICATION DIVISION.
PROGRAM-ID. HELLO-CBL.
DATA DIVISION.
WORKING-STORAGE SECTION.
DATA DIVISION.
01 NUM1 PIC S9(4) COMP VALUE 1
01 NUM2 PIC S9(4) COMP VALUE `1'
PROCEDURE DIVISION USING BY VALUE NUM1 NUM2
   .
DISPLAY NUM1 ' + ' NUM2 ' = ' SUM.
STOP RUN.
```

This would display:

```
1 + 1 = 2
```

The following code is for a program called "HouseCost" which takes the number of rooms in a house and the cost per room as variables and calculates how much it will cost to rebuild a house. The actual output is shown on the right:

This example shows that COBOL supports many data types such as numeric values, character fields and string values (known simply as strings). The strings are enclosed with double quotes while numeric values use single quotes. In COBOL there are two ways to control the execution of statements, Blocks and Procedures. The COBOL language supports the use of variables and constants, these can be assigned values by using reference numbers or by using a code number. If a code number is used, then it is called a formal procedure call. The use of formal procedures is limited in scope to the context in which it appears.

COBOL also supports Control Structures such as If Then Else and Switch-Case constructs.

Control structures are used to execute different sets of instructions based on Boolean expressions and data comparisons. They are often the first step taken in the execution of an operation or group of operations associated with a program statement.

BASIC was created by Bill Gates and Paul Allen in the early 1970s. The language was intended to be very simple and easy to use. BASIC was inspired by ALGOL-60 which was one of the first languages for computers developed.

Incompatible changes to BASIC syntax led to a restructuring of the language in its second version, resulting in a new SCRAMJET processor that eliminated incompatibilities. This new version of

BASIC was called "BASICA" and took its name from the original version, along with features for object-oriented programming and support for common file I/O operations.

In the late 1970s and early 1980s Microsoft BASIC became quite popular as a "home computer" language.

A special version of BASIC called Extended Color BASIC was also distributed with the Apple IIe in 1983. This version used the color capabilities of enhanced mode to provide colored text and graphics commands for things such as border drawing, animated sprites, and a special sound-playing routine.

In 1985 IBM released a new version of BASIC called Advanced BASIC designed for programmers. It had many new commands including support for structured programming, better string manipulation abilities, improved graphics features including support for true color (24-bit) graphics, and support for multitasking operating systems.

These BASIC keywords are statements that allow for branching based on the result of a comparison. For example, a program can branch based on whether the value of an expression is greater than or less than 199. If the expression's result is greater than or less than 199, one set of instructions will run. If it isn't, another set will run.

For example (in BASIC), if X = 219 then goto 5: if X<199 then goto 5:

The following code is for a simple BASIC program to find the highest numbers in an array of random numbers and display them on screen. It will display a random number between 1 and 999.

```
10 INPUT A$(1).
20 INPUT B$(1).
30 INPUT C$(1).
40 DO 50 I=2 TO 1000:READ A:IF (A>B) GOTO
70.
50 GOTO 30.
60 PRINT A.
70 NEXT I.
80 PRINT "The highest numbers are:".
90 END.
```

For example, a BASIC program can be written to print out the hourly cost of running a house furnace assuming $0.135 per hour to run it and that the furnace runs for 8 hours per day on average:

```
10 INPUT "HOURS" FURNACE RUNS PER DAY:B$(1).
20 INPUT "HOURS" FURNACE RUNS PER DAY:C$(1).
30 INPUT #WEEKS:A$(1).
40 INPUT #WEEKS:A$(2).
50 PRINT "HOURS" FURNACE RUNS PER DAY
60 FOR I=1 TO HOURS:READ B:A$(I) =
C$(I):NEXT I.
70 NEXT I.
80 IF (HOURS > 35) THEN PRINT "AFTER 35
HOURS"
90 END.
```

Now the program can be written to print out the hourly cost of running a house furnace assuming $0.09 per hour to run it and that the furnace runs for 8 hours per day on average:

```
10 INPUT "HOURS" FURNACE RUNS PER DAY:B$(1).
20 INPUT "HOURS" FURNACE RUNS PER DAY:C$(1).
30 INPUT #WEEKS:A$(1).
40 INPUT #WEEKS:A$(2).
50 PRINT "HOURS" FURNACE RUNS PER DAY
60 FOR I=1 TO HOURS:READ B:A$(I) =
C$(I):NEXT I.
70 NEXT I.
80 IF (HOURS > 35) THEN PRINT "AFTER 35
HOURS"
90 END.
```

In FORTRAN 77 and later, all comparisons with integer data types can be done in one step using the GO TO statement. The FORTRAN 77 format uses the same syntax as COBOL except it lacks support for string variables. This eliminates some of the difficulties found in earlier versions of BASIC including those that are specific to string data, such as copying the value of a character string into another variable when a command is issued to increment or to parse the value of a string variable.

For example, the following code would first use function MID$(x,y) to return the value in x to the left of y:

```
10 GO TO 20:20 INPUT A$(1)." at ";x;". at
";y.
20 GOTO 10:GO TO 10:10 INPUT MID$(A$,y);"
";x.
30 GO TO 40:40 INPUT MID$(B$,x);" at ";y.
40 END.
```

To display 'Hello, world!' in the title window of a graphical program, one can either write or use the operating system calls and functions.

In C++, the following piece of code illustrates how the GO TO statement is implemented in this language:

```
10 10 PRINT "Hello, world!" ;
15 15 GOTO 10;
```

The GO TO statement is part of the C programming language. Some other languages such as Java and JavaScript use pseudo-operators for conditional branching. In Java and JavaScript, the following piece of code illustrates how the GO TO statement is implemented in these languages:

```
10 10 System.out.println("Hello, world!");
15 15 return;
```

In C#, the following piece of code illustrates how the GO TO statement is implemented in this language:

```
20 [Print("Hello, world!")]()
25 [Return(value)]()
 #include <stdio.h>
int main()
#include <stdio.h>
int main() {
printf( "Hello, World!\n" );
return 0;
formula_1: Hello, World!
#include <stdio.h>
int main() {
printf( "Hello, World!\n" );
```

```
return 0; }
```

The GO TO statement is not generally a good idea in programming as it causes an unconditional branch to a line number that has been previously defined. This makes the program prone to errors when changes are made to the original code and introduces a control dependency between lines of code (there can be no more than one GOTO statement per each defined label).

Currently, some programming languages (including Python) implement control flow via single-line comments: that is to say, any code between those tags will be ignored by the program until removed with a special command like codice_2 or codice_3.

The programmer must have a clear understanding of the difference between data and its associated identifier. For example, if a person called "Smith" lives in town "Hackensack," then the name Smith is not data but is rather used to identify an individual. If we also know that Smith's age is 36 then we would say that 36 is data associated with (or pointing to) an individual called Smith. A variable or constant can be classified as either "data" or "abstract data.

Chapter 13

Cobol Utility Routines
for DBMS Interfacing

This is a list of the major Cobol utility routines and DBMS interfaces, which are used to interface with DBMS systems.

Cobol

Cobol is a programming language that has been primarily used in business applications, due to its flexibility and power. Cobol was first released in 1959 by Grace Hopper (inventor of COBOL), A. H. "Mike" McNair, J. Bamberger, and C. F. Burgum. Cobol was used to develop the first large business application on System/360, which was conducted by the New York State Department of Social Welfare.

DBMS

A database management system (DBMS) is a collection of programs that controls and maintains data stored in a computer system. The DBMS allows for users to create, retrieve, update and delete data from the database via applications using Structured

Query Language (SQL). Some popular DBMS are SQL Server, Oracle, IBM DB2, MySQL and PostGreSQL. All DBMS can be accessed through either proprietary or open source programming languages or through an interface called an API (Application Program Interface).

Cobol is an interpreted language and can only be used to create programs which explain the logic of specific business processes within a business as well as data processing.

Since its introduction, Cobol has been used to implement many of the early computer-based safety-critical systems because of its robustness and simplicity. These systems have included air traffic control, air traffic control tower automation, the ignition system for nuclear reactors and submarines, the main propulsion shaft for power plants, and many types of safety instrumented systems in motor vehicles. Today Cobol is still used by these industries and other industries that require reliability in an environment where failure is expensive.

A program in COBOL is written with a specific language syntax, and the programs are interpreted using the Cobol interpreter. This means that each line of code is run through the compiler and then executed after every modification. A typical Cobol program contains several thousands of lines of code. The following is an example program created with a blank computer:

This type of style may remind users that this would be perfect for writing computer programs to run on mainframes when COBOL was first created. However, today it is almost never used because most modern applications can use more than a dozen lines to accomplish the same task. Newer programming languages are created to make programming easier to do, and because of this they are often more efficient than COBOL.

The above example uses "READ", "MOVE" and "WRITE" statements which is common in the 1960s version of COBOL. The second line makes reference to a "FILE." A file is a storage container for data, or records, that are transmitted from the computer to the mainframe. A record is data about an individual involved in a business transaction such as a customer or employee. The actual values within that record would have been stored in the computer's memory. Each file is created, or first created, with a specific name and the record names that are within the file. Each file must be located within the same directory. The next line which sets a variable to "10". This variable is called a "CELL" (or Cell) in COBOL. A cell is an array of information that can be broken down into a number of rows and columns (see below). There are many variations to this syntax so users may write more elaborate programs by creating their own versions of "READ", "MOVE" and "WRITE".

COBOL systems are based on the concept of data tables which contain one or more files. Each individual record, or field, is called a "column" or "field" in COBOL. The lines of code that are entered into the computer are executed one after another, until the program they were written to is complete.

Both COBOL and DBMS systems use this same basic syntax; however, there are some differences between them. All basic commands in DBMS systems can be written in both COBOL and DBMS languages; however, there are some important differences that developers should be aware of during programming.

According to the "COBOL 2014 International Standard", column names must be unique within a table and column names must begin with ':'.

The following is a list of differences between COBOL and DBMS:

DBMS settings are saved in a database, other than the table itself. A record within the table, only ever has one column name. Records can have multiple columns; it is just that one of those columns is known as "primary" and another is the "foreign key" while some other columns don't have a foreign key at all. The SQL standard says that there can only be one primary key column (the 'id' column).

A data table in DBMS may contain more than one comma-separated values (CSV) file, but usually only one file. In COBOL, a data table may contain many files. In COBOL, the number of files in a data table may only be determined at run time.

While Cobol is used mainly to create business applications, it is also used in other systems including systems that control heavy machinery, automated teller machines (ATM) and point-of-sales (POS) terminals. Cobol was one of the first computer programming languages that were used to create air traffic control systems for aircraft. Today Cobol is still used for critical systems in industries such as banking and finance where mistakes could cause serious and costly problems.

COBOL is a business critical language and therefore, has many features that can be used to enhance program efficiency. For instance, tables can be stored in both main memory and on disk. This reduces the amount of time taken to transfer data from main memory to disk, which also reduces the amount of time needed to read the data from disk since it is no longer stored in memory. Another feature is that COBOL does not allow for any resource errors. The system will not allow an error to occur if a resource cannot be accessed or if it is held up in a queue.

In addition, COBOL supports two different types of variables: those used for local variables and those used for global variables. Global variables are for permanent storage of values, and local variables can be used for temporary storage of values that can be used later in the program.

COBOL also supports a couple of different types of subprograms called modules and entry points. A module is a type of subprogram that contains one or more procedures and they may be nested within other modules. An entry point is another type of subprogram that may also contain one or more procedures, but they cannot be nested within any other modules.

COBOL was designed to provide a balance between the business community's need to deal with business events as they happen and the programming developers' need to use standard programming language features. COBOL was one of the first languages to include an internal hierarchy with improved data processing functions as well as support for modular programming.

COBOL was designed to be used in a hierarchical system, which meant that different parts of the system would have different levels of priority. On machines with a limited amount of memory, this meant it could be more efficient to process more important events first, since this would reduce disk accesses and the likelihood of a crash caused by low memory conditions. The section on data management is designed to take advantage of COBOL's strengths and make it easier for developers to implement effective database management systems.

Chapter 14

Cobol Utility Routines
for Layout and Printing

Cobol has utilities for layout and printing. There are two other utilities, "CBLT" and "CBLTR", which simulate the console capabilities of other operating systems.

CBLT is the "classic" Cobol utility for layout, used in all versions of Cobol from the 1960s up to the 1980s. It was originally developed by Digital Equipment Corporation (DEC) and replaced "CBLR", DEC's other utility used for layout. CBLT was first introduced on the IBM 709/7090 mainframe, and has been backward-compatible with earlier models since then. The main purpose of CBLT was to provide a formatted screen that consisted of text characters, block characters, and binary data objects such as graphics or a cursor. The formatted screen was primarily intended for viewing by operator console devices, but could also be printed as needed. CBLT's primary advantage over CBLTR was that it had more features and was easier to use.

Originally written in assembly language for the DEC hardware, it has since been rewritten in various Cobol environments, such as the IBM System/360 and System/370, the Burroughs B5000, and more recently COBOL-based microcomputers. The original DEC version of CBLT is still used today by many companies and organizations throughout the world.

The latest version of CBLT can be obtained from Digital Equipment Corporation under a "GPL" license (open-source).

CBLT uses a "screen table" that is used to describe a screen's layout. The screen table (SCR) is a linear array of bytes, indexed by character position. Each byte in the SCR contains one character position and can hold one or more characters. The format of the SCR is:

"Size and type of the screen table".

size w bytes, where w is the number of characters per line.

characters to be displayed by the program, beginning at byte offset start (we will call this byte position start).

SCR {256 chars per line / 10 chars start}

So, for example, if we want a screen table with 10 characters per line and 256 lines, then the SCR data would look like this (in hexadecimal):

The next thing that the programmer must define is what goes in the character positions (i.e. what characters are displayed on each byte of the SCR). To do this, optional "field descriptors" can be used to define each position; these will also be stored in the SCR.

For example, if you wanted to print a line containing text in reverse video, you would use the following code:

WRITE file-id RECORD; <reverse line feed> TEXT; WRITE file-id RECORD; <carriage return>

This will cause COBOL to simulate printing the line of text back to front, like it would do on a typewriter (the key sequence for this operation is usually ESCAPE or CR). There are also two commands for doing centering - CENTR and CENTER.

COBOL also has a "FORMAT" command for specifying the format of a given SYSOUT, which is the standard way of creating formatted text in COBOL. There are many different kinds of format codes, but they are not very case sensitive, apart from the differentiating between upper-case and lower-case letters. A large number of different screen tables and a large number of COBOL program statements are needed to fully use the capabilities of CBLT. It is therefore often used alongside other utilities like CBLTR or CBLT.

CBLTR, or "Cobol Console Routines for Layout and Printing", was a utility to help maintain an empty screen table for printing in a Cobol environment. Unlike CBLT, it could create any sort of "scr$" (i.e., standard character screens) and could easily insert them into the table with the WRITE command. CBLTR did not have a "field descriptor" as such, but instead used the WRITE statement to insert special control characters into the SCR.

There is much confusion around CBLT and CBLTR. Capability wise, there is no difference between the two, but:

CBLTR was a much more popular utility than CBLT, although both were used extensively in all versions of Cobol up until the 1990s. CBLTR was introduced in COBOL-60 and replaced "CBLR" (DEC's other utility for lay outing). It was written in assembler language and has been backward compatible with previous models of IBM mainframe computers from that time.

Due to the large number of versions that have been in use for many years, CBLT and CBLTR are often referred to by their source code file names. The source code for CBLTR was "CBLTR.MAC" (for the IBM System/360) and "CBLTRS.MAC" (for the System/370). The file name for CBLT is "CBT.MAC" - this was originally written in assembly language, but has since been rewritten in Cobol (which is why it is called a "routine"). The original assembly language version of CBLT can still be found on many Digital Equipment Corporation mainframe computers today.

CBLT was used to print a line of text (e.g. the program output) to a low-speed printer and to create a formatted screen for viewing on a console terminal. CBLT also had utilities for plotting data, displaying graphics, and scrolling windows.

Some of the common uses for CBLT include:

There is still life in CBLTR; some organizations use it as an important utility for COBOL programmers. It is still used today because of its ability to maintain screens for printing, which CBLT does not offer. However, CBLTR is not always easy to come by due to the sheer number of different versions that have been produced over the years.

CBLT and CBLTR use a "screen table" that contains character positions and a "field descriptor" that gives information about each character position. The screen table (SCR) is a linear array of bytes, indexed by character position; each byte in this array contains one character position (i.e., where the text characters appear).

The size and type of the screen table is defined by two tags, or "fields", in the source code file "scr$". The tag describing the number of characters per line is named "w", while the tag describing how to interpret each byte position contains three fields. The three fields describe the "character position" defined by the writing program.

Chapter 15

Cobol Utility Routines
for String-handling

Following is an example of a COBOL string that can be used to illustrate how the different conditions affect string handling.

Different conditions and how they affect the handling of strings:

1. Is the string a blank (i.e., all characters in the string are alphabetic or 0's)

2. Is the string null (i.e., all characters in the string are 0's)

3. Is the string a long string (i.e., more than 64K characters)

4. Is the string a simple character string (i.e., less than 64K characters)

5. Is the "out" word wide or restricted? This can be affected by: 1) Null termination 2) Encoding 3) Character set 4) Locale 5) Remaining capabilities of out word 6 . Is end of line indicator required? 7 . Is end of file indicator required?

1. Is the string a blank

BLANKS IS DISTINCT FROM ALL 0'S. If a string has blanks, it can be considered as different than a null string. A null string is all 0's with no blanks. So, if you have a null string (all 0's) and you want to know if it's null or not, the following conditions are true: 1) > IS NULL or 2) = IS NULL. If the above conditions do not hold true, then the ASCII value of first non-blank character cannot be equal to 0 and the string is not truly null.

2. Is the string null

The following conditions are true when a string has all 0's and can be considered null: 1) > IS NULL or 2) = IS NULL. If any of the above conditions are not met, then the ASCII value of first non blank character cannot be equal to 0 and the string is not truly null.

3. Is the string a long string

If a non-null character string is greater than 64K characters in length, then it is considered to be in long-string form. All data items (including array elements) can only be assigned by using the four data modifier characters, that allow you to manipulate data items with long-strings (up to 32K elements). Any other combination of (program, field, data modifier) characters will produce an error message.

4. Is the string a simple character string

For convenience, for short character strings (less than 64K characters in length), it is better to store long-string data items and use a "program block" code to output such data correctly on the terminal screens. You can assign and manipulate the data values with the program block . . . displayed as ^D (for ^D place value) on the screen and , display as ^R (for ^R place value) and , displayed as ;(for ; place value - used as continuation character by CICS/TSO). These three combinations are also known as screen codes.

5. Is the "out" word wide or restricted? This can be affected by:

1) Null termination . . . . characters that are not permitted for the current COBOL standard are identified as null (in this case, ASCII value of ONE must not equal 0). 2) Encoding The character in a word parameter is used to display data values on a terminal screen and should therefore contain only characters that can be displayed on a terminal (i.e., it must not include the control characters). The restriction is that if the value of program parameter is greater than 64K, then it should be restricted prior to terminating null byte and any other characters that have no significance. For example, the character sequence "AB|CD" results in two null bytes being added (i.e., "ABCD" becomes "AB\0CD\0"). 3) Character set The character set determines how a value is displayed. For example, if you have an ASCII character set and values greater than 127 are displayed, they will be displayed as ESC followed by the characters - i.e., the screen code for an ESC is escape (ESC). 4) Locale The locale determines the language to be used to display other character sets with data values greater than 127. As an example, a Japanese-locale system (with double byte characters) will display ESC followed by characters if greater than 127. Also, you have to be aware that the only values that can be displayed through the

terminal code for COBOL programs are characters: 0, 1, 2 . . . 24. The ASCII value of 0 is used to display all numbers between 1 and 127. The ASCII value of 24 is used to display all letters. Other characters are used by COBOL programmers to specify the program and character registers (i.e., BPX0 or BX1W)

6. Remaining capabilities of out word

The out parameter is only 64K free for data items (up to 32K elements), plus there must be room for the string terminator double "0" (null character). If a character string has more than 32K elements, then the allowable characters are 64K characters (including 0 as a single element). However, you get to use the data modifier characters with these long-string data items.

7. Is end of line indicator required?

For COBOL programs, I/O functions are supported on the CICS and TSO terminals by using two data modifiers : . and !. The former is used if you want to use multiple output parameters or if the length of the string is greater than 32K or less than 64K. The latter is used if you want to use strings with less than 32K characters in length or assign multiple input parameters with one file position. For any string with less than 32K characters, you need to use the ! data modifier. You can assign screen codes and program blocks to I/O functions. Basically, screen codes and program blocks allow us to display data values on the terminal screen.

For example, the following is a string with one parameter: "abcdef" in which "abcdef" consists of 13 characters that are displayed as "abcdeg". The first letter of each word is displayed in uppercase (i.e., COBOL uses A for alphabetic characters). However, the second and third letter are not displayed (i.e., COBOL uses B for numeric characters), and so on up to the sixth character ("def"). In this case, you do not need the end-of-line indicator because there are less than 64K characters in this string. If the string were longer in length (i.e., greater than 64K characters), then the following code would display: "ABCDEF".

The output data item from this program is "abcdeg" . . . . The variable , which can only be used to store a single character value and not a character array, is automatically assigned the next available sequential position and cannot be re-assigned. The variable part of the out data item is assigned an ASCII value that corresponds to the first non blank character (i.e., ASCII 30 or 30H). The values in an ASCII character set were originally described by IBM as an 8-bit byte that includes codes for the alphabetic (upper and lower case), numeric, punctuation and special characters. The ASCII characters are in uppercase; non-ASCII characters (i.e., IBM EBCDIC) are in lowercase.

The ! data modifier is used to write a character field when the length is less than 64K or if it requires multiple parameters for output or if you want to write multiple data items with one file position (much like file level variables - that can only be used for output).

8. Is sign required?

A special code for the decimal point is used if it is required (i.e., if the number does not start with a number) to separate it from the

143

next digit for display on the screen: $ for positive and # for negative.

9. Is decimal position indicator required?

The decimal point indicator is used if a number ends with a decimal point (i.e., 5.8). The position can be left blank (i.e., 5,8). There are two exceptions:

You need to use the following codes:

1) "." Positive or negative, optional data modifier - i.e. 2,3,4,5. 2) "#" I/O function and -i.e., 0,1,2.

For example, the following is an ASCII program with one parameter: "abc" in which the first letter of each word is in uppercase while the second to fourth letters are not shown (i.e., COBOL uses A for alphabetic characters). The value of this parameter will be displayed as 'ABC'.

10. Is end of string indicator required?

The end-of-string indicator is used before the null character (00H) because it helps to determine if a string ends with a parameter that has been assigned a data modifier (e.g. 00H). The end-of-string indicator is also used before the character string terminator, which is specified by a period (.).

11. Is end of file indicator required?

The end of file indicator is used before any byte beyond the last byte in a file. This includes return codes, although it can be used before any I/O function program block or data modifier character that follows immediately after the last byte of a data item. It can also be used in combination with the variables and symbols that occur in upper or lower case within an output string: . . . . . # etc.

12. Is carriage return required?

The carriage return keeps the program from going to the next line on the screen. It also does not advance the current line pointer to a new line. The value of a carriage return is 13H.

13. Is line feed required?

The line feed keeps the program from going to the next character on a new line on the screen. It also advances the current character pointer to a new character in an output string. The value of a line feed is 10H.

14. Is form feed required?

The form feed is used in combination with the PROMPTs. The program uses a form feed for data strings (1 to 32K or 128) and variable names. A form feed does not include the terminal cursor location information from the text editor (i.e., what was written on the screen). It also does not advance to a new line within a program, but it can be used in conjunction with a new line key item if you want to move between lines in an I/O function program block. The value of this prefix is FFH.

15. Is CR/LF character pair required?

The CR and LF characters are used as terminators between strings. If the string is less than 32K characters in length, the CR is optional - you need to use only the LF. The value of a CR/LF pair is 11H.

16. Is line feed character pair (U+000A) required?

The line feed character pairs are used for purposes other than string termination; they are not part of the ASCII standard. The first example below shows multiple parameters within one file position: "registrar" . . . . The second example below shows multiple data modifiers within one file position: "abc" . . . . The third example below shows how to use a line feed character pair to continue a long number string: $12,345.67 . . .

17. Is record terminator required?

The record terminator is used when a program writes to sequential files or records where the length of each record can vary in length. It is also used by the I/O subroutine functions that are used as an alternative to the direct access method (I/O, print and write). It consists of 18H between each byte within a file position or 12H after each byte within an I/O function program block that follows the last byte within a data item.

Chapter 16

Cobol Utility Routines
for Text and Table Processing

C BRT/CUT is an adaptation of the Cobol utility routines for text and table processing which is similar in many respects to COBOL, but with some key simplifications for use in cases where a simple string manipulation function is needed."

This COBOL document provides information about CURT or Cobol Utility Routines for Text and Table Processing. This document is especially helpful if you need a program that works like COBOL but can be used on non-COBOL systems. The documentation provides details on what the text means and shows how to use CURT. It also includes other functions like JCL, a collection of commands that would be used in automation programs.

The language was "a simplification of the ANSI COBOL standard," and drew on both earlier languages like COMTRAN and FLOW-MATIC, and later ones such as IDG.

COBOL is a programming language that has been around since the 1950s. It was designed to be used for business data processing, and because of this it has commands for handling files, character string manipulation, and specific math operations. These routines are called "utilities". This blog post will go over these COBOL utilities in detail.

Introduction to COBOL Utilities Part One: File Manipulation

There are utility programs which handle file input/output (I/O). The ACCEPT program handles files for input. OUTPUT programs handles output of data from the program to various devices such as screens, printers, or other storage media like disk drives or tapes.

Introduction to COBOL Utilities Part Two: Integer Arithmetic and String Manipulation

Integer arithmetic is the basic arithmetic behind all COBOL programs. This is done with the COUNT, COMPARE and BINARY functions. String manipulation involves using operations such as CAR, CDR, UDR and MID.

Introduction to COBOL Utilities Part Three: Basic Date Processing

In addition to integer arithmetic there are some routines that process dates. You can do this with the DATE function in conjunction with an explicit TIME value or you can use the DATE function as part of a CALENDAR transaction.

Introduction to COBOL Utilities Part Four: The DD Statement

When you write COBOL programs you need to call upon the operating system. This happens in the form of dialogs, or DD statements. The DD statement describes the action that is going to be taken when a user selects a particular option from the dialog. Some of these actions are fairly straightforward, like DEVICE or STRING, but there are some more complicated ones as well. An example would be DD DISPLAY when the user types in "Control-D". This tells the operating system to display whatever text has been entered so far. There is also a TIMER which forces an action after time intervals have elapsed without event.

Introduction to COBOL Utilities Part Five: The TIME Procedure

One of the more complicated utilities is the TIME procedure. This is called within every DD statement. It tells how often the operating system is going to be running its event service by making that a parameter of a DD statement. The operating system determines this value based upon the environment in which it is run. The TIME function also has some variables available to it so you can get more precise information about what the operating system will look like at any given duration.

Introduction to COBOL Utilities Part Six: Control Statement Processing

The COBOL language does not have a block structure like C does, but does have some control structures that can simulate blocks. One of those is the IF statement. An IF statement must have exactly one expression following it. This expression can be a literal value, like 17 or the character 'o' for an OR logical test and the character "S" for a SET statement. The COBOL language also has another control statement called the DO WHILE loop which acts much like a loop in C.

Introduction to COBOL Utilities Part Seven: Record Processing Tools

COBOL provides the ability to manipulate data in a variety of records, but there are some special tools which allow you to process them even better. You can use data check or validation to ensure records have the correct number of fields and that their contents are valid. Also, there are some tools for working with sequential files. In COBOL you can perform sequential file operations like reading a record, writing a record or doing both at once.

Introduction to COBOL Utilities Part Eight: Date and Time Processing

The TIME procedure has variables which allow you to get information about the system's environment. These values are important when it comes to processing dates and times. The system variable CURRENT_DATE returns the current year, month and day when run at any time during the session. CURRENT_TIME also returns a time, but this value is the number of seconds that have elapsed since 00:00:00 GMT, January 1, 1900. To convert this to a standard time value you need to add the TIMEZONE system variable.

Introduction to COBOL Utilities Part Nine: Mathematical Operations

The COBOL programming language has three different statements specifically for mathematical operations. The SIN function returns the sine of a given number and the COS function returns the cosine of any given angle in radians. The TAN function allows you to find tangent (half-sine) values as well.

Introduction to COBOL Utilities Part Ten: Exercises

So what can you do if you don't know how to program in COBOL? First, you can always order a book to help with your COBOL programming. Where you go from there is completely up to you. There are plenty of sites on the Internet where people share their own code for solving problems, or where they offer hints on how to improve your programming skills. Experimenting in your free time will help get you ready for when it is time to actually write some code of your own.

The good news is that the language itself really isn't that difficult and once you learn it, the rules and syntax are fairly simple. The many utilities available will help you accomplish your programming goals, but it makes sense to learn the basics first. You don't need to be an expert, or even know all the language details, but it is important to master the basics first.

Chapter 17

Cobol Program-Generation Utilities

The main issue in the research of Cobol is to identify and analyze the tools and techniques for decomposing a large computer application in to smaller programs. The procedural language COBOL is often used in this process. The main goal of these tools is to generate the smaller programs faster and better and to improve on the processes or techniques used for decomposition. Some scripts are even integrated into the Cobol compiler for producing code.

Computer hardware, software, and systems have become increasingly complex over time, resulting in large amounts of COBOL source code that are difficult to maintain efficiently. This problem can occur when the software is constructed from many different modules. In contemporary applications it is rare that all modules are linked into one large executable application; instead, many small applications (called "components") will be linked together to form a larger whole. Various approaches to software reuse have been proposed (as has been the case with other languages) and various approaches to source code modularization have been adopted. In this approach, source code is divided into separate modules, exposing the public interfaces of these modules for use in other programs. Once this is complete, the reverse engineering process can begin. The ultimate goal is a high-level design that can be transformed into a formal COBOL specification for use in program generation.

An alternative approach is to employ code generator tools, which provide a high-level language interface construct for describing high-level algorithms and functionality. Tools like these can generate substantial amounts of code from a high-level specification. Although this approach has been widely used in the field of software engineering, it has not seen wide proliferation outside software engineering circles due to a lack of documentation outlining how these tools work. Without this documentation, it can be difficult to use these tools for the purpose for which they were designed, namely to generate COBOL code that is more maintainable.

The application of code generator tools to the decomposition of large COBOL applications in to smaller components can be difficult. Although there are many such tools available, they are not widely known and are not always easy to use. Additionally, few such tools provide a specification language similar to that used in UML, which is typically used for specifying high level models of a software system. This makes it difficult or impossible to produce a formal specification that could then be used for the generation of automated code. Some tools have attempted to address this issue, but they are not widely documented, nor is there consensus on how they should be used.

While the utility of such tools remains hotly debated within the software engineering community as a whole, many researchers are in agreement that tools can help with the process of decomposition. However, once these tools have been employed to develop high-level specification (a UML model) many issues remain that must be addressed before this specification can then be transformed into actual working code. At present there is no consensus on exactly how this transformation should be carried out. Further, there is no consensus about the method for transforming a formal specification into an actual working program. Few tools exist that perform this transformation. Even when these tools do exist, they are typically not documented well enough to allow them to be used effectively by those who are unfamiliar with them.

The use of automated code generators is still a controversial topic within the field of computer science. The debate between proponents and critics of automatic code generation is at its most fierce in the COBOL programming community, where few such tools exist with any documentation on how they work or even proof that they generate valid code at all.

One of the main issues is the lack of any consensus on exactly how code generators work. This, in turn, stems from the fact that there are no definitive books or papers describing exactly how these tools work and what their inner workings are. Academic researchers have published papers on source code transformation and automatic code generation, but little or no documentation exists explaining how to use these tools in practice. This can be attributed in part to a general lack of interest in automatic code generation outside the narrow band of software engineering research. As a result, many such tools were never documented or were deprecated before their utility could be proven via peer review by people who understood them.

There are, however, some commercial applications of automatic code generation. One such application is the software known as The Harrogate Software Factory. This tool was originally developed by David J. Cargill and has been used to generate COBOL source code by a wide variety of different organizations including the University of Missouri at Columbia and the Billings Clinic Medical Group Foundation in Oregon.

Cargill also consulted with Dr. John R. Betts at the University of Missouri, who was developing an automated system to convert high level models into code in the 1980s and 1990s. Betts was one of the most vocal critics of automated code generation and didn't see how automatic code generation, as Cargill defined it, would ever be useful or acceptable. Betts considered it a form of "code doping", in which some developers would try to inject more features into their programs than was necessary.

There are a number of known issues with the use of such automated code generators; some of these impacts should be considered before using such tools:

Most current commercial COBOL code generators are not capable of generating very large programs. Some say this is because these tools are not designed to handle this level complexity, but others suggest that it is due to the fact that current COBOL tools do not work well with high level source (or any source for that matter).

The core of the Harrogate system is the Open Cobol Utilities Library, which contains a set of libraries used by all three of the other components when generating COBOL code. The Open Cobol Facilitator uses this library to generate COBOL source code from a UML model. The output it generates can be interpreted by either the Open Cobol Compiler or by an interpreter contained in another Harrogate component called the Open Cobol Interpreter.

Appendix A

ASCII/EBCDIC Conversion Tables

Tables

Tables are fundamental to programming, and for this reason, there isn't a single computer language that does not offer the facility. The reason for the facility being so common is that they simplify so many tasks that it is inconceivable to program without using tables. We are all acquainted with tables in one form or another. We can have a bus or train timetable. We can also have a table, which most of us have seen at one time or another, which is simply a list of names or a list of numbers. Basically a table is a list of identical items. In storage each of these items will lie one adjoining the other.

Processing Lists

We will consider an example involving a very simple application where we have data coming in from the console. The data will consist of a number, between 1 and 12 for the month, and a monetary value reflecting the sales for the month. We will add the

157

sales for the month to the existing value as each branch provides similar figures.

```
01  W20-mth-sales.
05  W20-mth           pic S9(02).
05  W20-mth-sales     pic S9(05).
```

Because the programmer does not know how to use tables, his solution bypasses the use of tables. His definition for the fields to be updated is:

A List of Fields	
01 W30-yearly-sales.	
05 W30-jan	pic S9(05).
05 W30-feb	pic S9(05).
05 W30-mar	pic S9(05).
05 W30-apr	pic S9(05).
05 W30-may	pic S9(05).
05 W30-jun	pic S9(05).
05 W30-jul	pic S9(05).
05 W30-aug	pic S9(05).
05 W30-sep	pic S9(05).
05 W30-oct	pic S9(05).
05 W30-nov	pic S9(05).
05 W30-dec	pic S9(05).
Figure 14.01	

We then need a string of if statements to determine the month that needs to be updated.

A List of Ifs
if W20-mth = "jan"
add W20-mth-sales to W30-jan
else if W20-mth = "feb"
add W20-mth-sales to W30-feb
else if W20-mth = "mar"
add W20-mth-sales to W30-mar
else if W20-mth = "apr"
add W20-mth-sales to W30-apr
else if W20-mth = "may"
add W20-mth-sales to W30-may
else if W20-mth = "jun"
add W20-mth-sales to W30-jun
else if W20-mth = "jul"
add W20-mth-sales to W30-jul
else if W20-mth = "aug"
add W20-mth-sales to W30-aug
else if W20-mth = "sep"

```
        add W20-mth-sales to W30-sep

else if  W20-mth = "oct"

    add W20-mth-sales to W30-oct

else if  W20-mth = "nov"

    add W20-mth-sales to W30-nov

else if  W20-mth = "dec"

    add W20-mth-sales to W30-dec.
```

Appendix B

Metric Conversion Factors

This is a list of metric conversions in the code for COBOL programs.

The format is "base-10" or "base-n" where n is an integer.

The value of 10 is given the name "decimal".

For example, one unit is given the name "meter".

It would be written as Meter-10 to indicate that it's a decimal number.

The value of 11 is given the name "pica".

For example, one unit is given the name "centimeter".

It would be written as Centimeter-11 to indicate that it's a pica number.

The value of 12 is given the name "inch".

For example, one unit is given the name "inch".

It would be written as Inch-12 to indicate that it's in inches, or 12 units long.

Note: The actual size or scale of inch or centimeter may vary. They will often be less than 1/25th of an inch.

I. Basic Conversions

A. From metric to English system: Multiply by $10 ** 2$

B. From English system to metric: Divide by $10 ** 2$

II. Volume Conversions (Approximate)

A. A liter is 1000 cubic centimeters or 100 cubic decimeters or 1000 milliliters or 1000 cubic millimeters, therefore a gallon is 3785 liters and a pint is 1637 milliliters or 1637 cubic centimeters, etcetera. The chart below gives the approximate conversion factors for other units of volume as well as their equivalent in liters and gallons:

```
1 quart = 0.946 liter = 1/32 gallon = 0-3579
cc ft.
1 pint = 1.946 liter = 1/8 gallon = 0-47317
cc ft.
1 cup = 0.2446 liter = 0-113579 cc ft.
1 fluid ounce (fl oz) = 29.338 milliliters
1 teaspoon (tsp) = 5.678 mililiters
```

1 fluid dram (fd) – dram being an old term for teaspoon – is 1/16 of a fluid ounce, or 3 teaspoons and is abbreviated fl dr -a dram being the old word for "dram" liquid measure and sometimes written as such:). The dram being 1/8 fluid ounce.

162

B. A cubic centimeter is the volume of a cube with each edge one centimeter in length and thus a liter is the volume of a cube with each edge 10 centimeters and a cubic foot, at 12 inches per side, is 0.0283 cubic meters or 283 cubic decimeters, again the chart:

```
1 cu.ft = 0.0283 m3 (approximate) = 2831 cc
ft.
1 mililiter (ml) = 0-061181 cu ft
1 teaspoon (tsp) = 5 ml = 0-179538 cu in.
1 dram (dram) = 1/16 fl oz = 5.68 cm3
1 fl.oz = 29.344 ml
```

C. In metric units (for computing purposes), the following conversion factors are useful:

1 centimeter in length is equal to 0.019937037037037037037 cm.

1 meter in length is equal to 10 decimeters or 100 centimeters or 1000 millimeters and therefore 1 centimeter has a value of 1 / 100 x 0.019937037037037037037 meters; thus a meter is 1000 m, 10 meters is 101.

Appendix C

Numeric Precision
in Cobol Language Codes

Many Cobol programs contain numeric precision (also called decimal mode) in Cobol language codes. Numeric precision is the number of digits that follow a radix point. The radix point occurs at the first digit position and indicates which base should be used in the calculation.

For example, 10/100 would be written as 0b0 (base 10), and 22/100 as 0o22 (base 2). Though most modern programming languages do not require numeric precision, many older ones do. For example, Fortran does not have decimal-mode support because it was designed to exchange data with scientists and engineers who had very limited computer experience. The lack of numeric precision has a major impact on the performance of Fortran programs. Newer Cobol compiler technology does not currently detect numeric precision errors in the language codes.

Example: If a report for the 15th grade was due on the 15th, the code would be written as:

SOUP uses its own numbering system. For example, SOUP-0023 is the classroom number 4 (00001). SOUP-0024 to SOUP-0039 are numbered in order. SOUP-0030 and above are "unused". A procedure to return all numbers from 1 through 960 would be as follows:

This only works because Numeric Precision is zero in Cobol language codes. The correction would be:

To make the program more readable a display routine would be added:

The "32" in the second line is not a number but is interpreted as a Numeric Precision error. This can be avoided by using the sign "=".

Example: The rounding of an amount of $1,352.57 to two decimal places is performed as follows. The roundoff error will be about 0.3% (910/1,352.57).:

SOUP uses its own numbering system. For example, SOUP-0023 is the classroom number 4 (00001). SOUP-0024 to SOUP-0039 are numbered in order. SOUP-0040 to SOUP-0063 are "unused". The procedure would be:

This only works because Numeric Precision is zero in Cobol language codes. A correction would be:

To make the program more readable a display routine would be added:

The "32" in the second line is not a number but is interpreted as a Numeric Precision error. This can be avoided by using the sign "=".

Example: The rounding of an amount of 1552.57 to two decimal places is performed as follows. The roundoff error will be about 0.3% (1552/1552.57).:

SOUP uses its own numbering system. For example, SOUP-0023 is the classroom number 4 (00001). SOUP-0024 to SOUP-0039 are numbered in order. SOUP-0040 to SOUP-0063 are "unused". The procedure would be:

This only works because Numeric Precision is zero in Cobol language codes.

Appendix D

Error Messages and Return Codes

Here are some common error messages and return codes you might encounter when using COBOL:

- File IO error 202: Unable to open file "filename".
- FILE I/O error 203: Unable to close file "filename".
- FILE I/O error 204: Unable to write into file "filename".
- FILE I/O error 205: Unable to read from file "filename".
- FILE I/O error 206: Unable to flush output file buffer.
- File not found message.
- FILE I/O error 301: Unable to rename file "filename".
- FILE I/O error 302: Unable to delete file "filename".
- Unknown COBOL class message.
- File IO error 401: Unable to open file "filename". Page 1 of 5 1 234 ...